Bank On Yourself

Bank On Yourself

*The Life-Changing Secret to Growing and
Protecting Your Financial Future*

Pamela G. Yellen

DA CAPO PRESS
A Member of the Perseus Books Group

Designed by Hespenheide Design
Set in 11.5 point Adobe Garamond by the Perseus Books Group

Library of Congress Cataloging-in-Publication Data

Yellen, Pamela G.
    Bank on yourself : the life-changing secret to growing and protecting your
    financial future / Pamela G. Yellen.
    p. cm.
    ISBN: 978-1-59315-496-7 (hardcover : alk. paper)
    1. Finance, Personal. 2. Retirement income—Planning. I. Title.
    HG179.Y45 2009
    332.024—dc22

                                                    2008052383

First Vanguard Press edition 2009
First Vanguard Press paperback edition 2010
First Da Capo Press paperback edition 2014

ISBN 978-1-59315-566-7 (paperback)
ISBN 978-0-7867-4534-0 (e-book)

Published by Da Capo Press
A Member of the Perseus Books Group
www.dacapopress.com

Da Capo Press books are available at special discounts for bulk purchases in the U.S. by corporations, institutions, and other organizations. For more information, please contact the Special Markets Department at the Perseus Books Group, 2300 Chestnut Street, Suite 200, Philadelphia, PA 19103, or call (800) 810-4145, ext. 5000, or e-mail special.markets@perseusbooks.com.

10 9 8

For Larry Hayward,

my husband, best friend, and the greatest love of my life

CONTENTS

When the original manuscript of this book was completed just over one year ago, both our financial system and the entire economy were falling off a cliff. As I write this Note in mid-December 2009—two weeks before a tumultuous decade comes to a close during which our nation suffered through *two* devastating market crashes—there are a few tentative signs that a recovery may be at hand. But financial stability is anything but certain, as government spending soars, unemployment remains stubbornly high, tax hikes loom, and the dollar declines.

And while the S&P 500 may have rebounded by a dizzying 64 percent after the worst stock market meltdown since the Great Depression, it is **still almost 25 percent below where it was nearly a decade ago**. And that doesn't even factor in 28 percent inflation during this period! You could have done better stuffing your money in your mattress and skipped the sleepless nights.

Many people were also counting on the equity in their homes to help fund their retirement. Yet today, the average home price is **down almost 30 percent** from its peak in 2005, foreclosures are at record highs, and 16 million homeowners have *no* equity to count on, because they owe more than their homes are worth.

The idea of having a comfortable, worry-free retirement has become a distant dream for many—even for those who did "all the right things" that Wall Street and the financial gurus told them to do.

In a desperate search for investments that *might* help them recoup their losses, some people are buying gold, currency, and commodities. Most have no idea that, historically, these assets have jumped up and down like a ten-year-old on a new trampoline. Case in point: Gold has been hitting record highs, yet most people I've surveyed aren't aware that *it would have to rise by another $1,000 an ounce, just to have the same purchasing power that it had 30 years ago*.

How quickly we forget that today's hot investment is almost always tomorrow's loser.

While the "experts" lamented that there was "no place to hide" during the financial crisis, none of the hundreds of thousands of people who use Bank On Yourself® lost a penny in their plans when the stock and real estate markets crashed. Their plans *never skipped a single beat* as both their principal and gains not only remained intact, but *also continued growing by a guaranteed and predictable amount*. (To see proof, visit: **www.BankOnYourself.com**)

Credit is still extremely tight for both businesses and consumers, underscoring just how little control we have when we have to rely on other people's money. Yet, for those who are using the Bank On Yourself method—which has enabled them to become their *own* source of financing—the only question they need to answer to gain access to capital is, "How much do I want?"

The $100,000 cash reward I offered to the first person who could show they use a different product or strategy that can match or beat Bank On Yourself still remains unclaimed. If you think you're up to the eye-opening **$100,000 Challenge**, visit **www.BankOnYourself.com**.

Bank On Yourself is a turbo-charged variation of a financial asset that has *increased in value during every single market crash* and in *every* period of economic boom *and* bust for more than a century.

For these reasons—and many more you will discover in these pages—Bank On Yourself may well be the ultimate financial security blanket in both good times and bad. Read on to discover how this time-tested method is helping folks of all ages, incomes, and backgrounds reach a wide variety of short-term and long-term personal and financial goals and dreams. And find out how you, too, could have a nest-egg you can predict and count on.

PREFACE

It's been said that if you do what everyone else is doing, you will achieve only average results.

As I write this in late 2008, it's become increasingly clear that, when it comes to financial and retirement planning, following the crowd simply isn't working. You needn't look very far for proof of that.

As a consultant to tens of thousands of financial advisors, I have been exposed to literally hundreds of financial products, strategies, and concepts, many of which were touted as sure bets for growing wealth. After careful investigation, most proved to be worthless, or even hazardous to my financial health.

However, I continued searching for a way to grow wealth predictably, without losing sleep, and without having to worry that our investments might tank just when my husband and I were ready to retire. Or worse, discovering after we'd *already* retired that the interest and investment income we were counting on had been drastically reduced.

I came to the conclusion that an appropriate financial product or method had to meet three basic criteria: it had to be brain-dead simple —simple to implement, and pretty much able to operate on autopilot. After all, I already have a more-than-full-time job I love; I have no interest in spending my leisure time analyzing stock charts or pounding the pavement searching for the perfect real estate investment.

My second requirement was that it had to be virtually foolproof and require no luck, skill, or guesswork—something almost anyone can do.

My third and final criterion was that it must actually work—so we'd have confidence that our nest egg would grow *safely* every year and wouldn't go backward.

I found this combination of requirements—and so much more— when I finally learned about Bank On Yourself®. The surprise was that the financial tool used for it had been right under my nose all along. This book is about a unique and little-known twist on a financial vehicle that's existed for more than one hundred years that, when combined with a mind-bending financial principle, lets you get back the money you spend on big-ticket items, plus the interest you pay to financial institutions. All those dollars you recapture can create a richer lifestyle for you now and, at the same time, fund a retirement you can truly count on.

I believe Bank On Yourself is the most powerful money secret of all. But I'll let you be the judge of that.

PART ONE

Financial Secrets "They" Don't Want You to Know

CHAPTER 1

Myths, Lies, and a New Way to Prosperity

The problem in America isn't so much what people don't know; the problem is what people think they know that just ain't so.

—WILL ROGERS

I'm going to make a very bold statement that I can—and will—back up in this book: the American public has been brainwashed into believing they must accept risk, volatility, and unpredictability to grow wealth and have a comfortable lifestyle in retirement.

There *is* a proven financial vehicle that can give you the peace of mind you seek and deserve, and provides a solution to most of the financial challenges and crises we face in our country today.

Furthermore, the financial vehicle that makes this possible comes with an *extraordinary* combination of advantages and guarantees, not the least of which is that it allows you to get back every penny you pay for major purchases, so you can enjoy life's luxuries *today* while growing your nest egg safely and predictably for tomorrow.

Unfortunately, for reasons you'll soon discover, you most likely *won't* hear about this from your financial advisor, stockbroker, CPA, banker, or credit card companies—which is why I felt compelled to write this book.

I'll reveal the reasons why the vast majority of Americans now feel their chances of having a secure financial future and a relatively comfortable retirement look increasingly slim. And I'll show you a surprisingly simple way to turn the direction of financial energy in your life *toward* you so you can leap ahead financially, even if that seems unimaginable to you now.

When you've read just the first few chapters, I think you'll already agree this book contains the most important financial information you've ever come across.

How to Win the Money Game

This book reveals a little-known but time-tested and proven wealth-building financial tool that can enable you to:

> ➤ Have a rock-solid financial plan and a predictable retirement income that can last as long as you do (chapters 4, 6, and 7)
> ➤ Turn your back on the stomach-churning twists and turns of the stock and real estate markets (chapters 3, 7, and 9)
> ➤ Make major purchases the Spend and Grow Wealthy® way so you can get back the entire purchase price of your cars, vacations, and other big-ticket items, and change the flow of money in your life from cash out to cash in (chapters 2, 3, and 6)
> ➤ Stop choosing between enjoying life's luxuries today and saving for tomorrow—it's possible to enjoy the things you want, *without* robbing your nest egg (chapters 2 and 9)
> ➤ Become your own source of financing so you have access to capital when you need it, and so you can recapture the interest and finance charges you'd otherwise pay to credit card companies and financial institutions, and reduce or eliminate the control those institutions have over your life (chapters 2, 8, 10, and 11)
> ➤ Use the money growing in your plan to buy things or to invest in anything you want, while your plan continues to grow as though you never touched a dime of it—your money can literally do double duty for you (chapters 6, 8, and 11)
> ➤ Pay for college for your kids or grandkids without going broke (chapter 10)
> ➤ Have the peace of mind that comes with knowing you won't have to rely on an employer or on failing government programs for your financial security (chapters 1, 6, and 7)

All of this—and much more—is possible, and more than 100,000 Americans are already doing it. You'll meet some of them and hear their stories in these pages.

You *don't* need any advanced skills or specialized knowledge, you won't have to worry about picking the right stocks, funds, or other investments, and it takes only a few minutes a year to implement and monitor.

Almost anyone can use this method to help reach his or her financial goals and dreams, from the business executive to the grocery store clerk, the physician, nurse, dentist, or chiropractor to the sales professional or computer analyst, the already wealthy to those who live from paycheck to paycheck.

It's not magic, although the benefits you get do seem quite magical. It does take some patience and discipline. However, if you have those traits and don't live beyond your means, the results can be remarkable.

The Ultimate Money Secret

Many Americans could have a nest egg several times larger than they would otherwise have, simply by buying their cars the Spend and Grow Wealthy way I reveal in chapters 2 and 6, rather than by financing or leasing them. This method even beats paying cash for things by a long shot. After all, most people will spend hundreds of thousands of dollars or more just on their cars over their lifetime, and it's money they'll never see again. I'm going to show you a way to recapture those dollars and turn them into wealth, without gambling your hard-earned money in the stock or real estate markets, or in other risky investments.

Bank On Yourself lets you dramatically
increase the wealth you could have
available to use and enjoy throughout your
lifetime, without gambling your hard-
earned money in stocks, real estate, or
other risky investments.

And you can do the same thing with the money you now spend on vacations, home repairs and remodels, college educations, business equipment, or any other major purchase, exponentially increasing the wealth you could have available to use and enjoy throughout your lifetime.

Although the financial vehicle used to give you all these benefits has stood the test of time for well over one hundred years, you almost certainly won't hear about it from your financial planner or advisor or your CPA. And, for reasons that are probably obvious, Wall Street, your banker, and finance, leasing, and credit card companies are desperately hoping you don't find out about it.

As you might have guessed from the title of this book, I call the method that makes all of this possible Bank On Yourself (or B.O.Y.) because it allows you to become your own source of financing and to turn your back on the banks, finance, and credit card companies that want to lend you money, and even the mortgage lenders that want to apply most of your monthly payments to interest. It also frees you from relying on Social Security, the government, or an employer for financial security.

An Accidental Discovery

I stumbled across B.O.Y. almost by accident. I am *not* a financial advisor, CPA, or attorney. But as a business-building consultant who has worked with over thirty thousand financial advisors since 1990, I've been exposed to just about every financial product, tool, concept, and method for growing wealth. Over the years, I've investigated hundreds of them, ranging from the ordinary to the exotic, only to find most weren't even worth the paper they were printed on.

Of those that did pass my scrutiny, most turned out to be disappointments when I implemented them.

All this learning the hard way came at a costly financial and emotional price. One financial vehicle that came highly touted cost me every penny I put into it, and then some.

Disappointed with the results we were getting when we were managing our investment program ourselves, my husband and I hired three of the country's top investment and planning firms in succession over a period of a decade to manage our retirement account.

A blindfolded monkey throwing darts could probably have done as well or better than the pricey experts we hired to manage our retirement accounts.

These companies were always on the lists of the country's top-ten financial planners and asset managers. They all charged hefty fees and *all three* of them *lost* us money during a period that included the longest-running bull market in history! I began to wonder whether a blindfolded monkey throwing darts could have done as well, or better.

My husband, Larry, and I would be in the same boat as so many Americans today—wondering if we'd *ever* be able to retire, and what we'd have to go without to do it—had it not been for one of my financial advisor clients mentioning a seminar he'd attended. That's where he heard about a way ordinary people could become their own source of financing, get back the cost of major purchases, and grow wealth safely—without the unpredictability and volatility of the stock and real estate markets.

I was intrigued, to say the least. It sounded too good to be true, but luckily I decided to keep an open mind. I spent months investigating it and I couldn't poke any holes in it. Then I implemented it myself to see if it would really work.

The Spend and Grow Wealthy Way to Make Major Purchases

As of this writing in late 2008, my husband and I have used the B.O.Y. method to get back the full purchase price of our last four cars, along with the interest charges we *used* to pay to finance and leasing companies . . . and *then* some. And we've already laid the foundation to be able to use this method to get back the cost of each of our two family cars, every four years or so, for the rest of our lives.

A few years back, we bought three time-share weeks at five-star resorts in Scottsdale, Arizona, and San Diego. Not only are the interest payments we would have made to a bank to finance these vacation homes going into our own pocket, we are on schedule to get back the full price just seven years after purchasing them, along with some extra "profit."

When my husband landed in the hospital for emergency quadruple bypass heart surgery, we got slammed with over $15,000 of medical bills that our health insurance didn't cover. Although unreimbursed medical expenses account for 50 percent of bankruptcies, for us, it simply meant borrowing from our B.O.Y. plan to pay off Larry's medical bills in full, and then paying ourselves back on our own payment schedule, with no finance charges going into the pockets of banks or credit card companies. By doing this, we actually ended up getting back every penny we'd paid for those medical expenses *and*, to our relief and astonishment, we even made a profit on the deal!

When we put in the home theater my husband had been dreaming about for years, we financed it the same way. We didn't pay one single penny of interest to a bank or credit card company for it, and within two years, we had recovered *all* the money we paid for it. We indulge our passion for collecting fine art the same way.

Unlike most parents or grandparents who are paying for college with money that *could* have gone to enrich their retirement lifestyle, my husband and I are using B.O.Y. to finance college tuition for our two grandchildren. Like everything else we finance through our Bank On Yourself plan, we'll get back all that money, too.

When I need to buy equipment for my business, I finance it the same way.

 Key Concept

> While the value of our mutual funds, real estate, and other investments has careened violently like an out-of-control roller coaster through the years, we *can't wait* to open our statements for our B.O.Y. plans—they *always* have good news and *never* any of those ugly surprises. And the news just keeps getting better every year!

We've never lost a wink of sleep over our Bank On Yourself plans. Never had the sickening feeling in the pit of our stomachs that you get with investments you have no control over and that put your financial security at risk. *Our B.O.Y. plans have continued growing, even when the stock market, real estate, and other investments are plunging.*

The "Easy-as-Shooting-Fish-in-a-Barrel" Retirement Plan

With a B.O.Y. plan, you can know the minimum value of your plan and the minimum annual income you can count on when you're ready to start taking it. To me, this is the difference between "hoping" and "knowing" how much money you could have in retirement. Do you think that difference could give you the peace of mind that's missing from most financial and retirement planning strategies?

It lets you shut out all the noise about the whipsawing stock and real estate markets and other investments. It's hard for many people to imagine what it's like to be able to do that. I know it was for my husband and me, before we discovered Bank On Yourself. But the peace and calm you feel when you *know* you have a rock-solid financial plan in place is indescribable.

Once I knew from personal experience the extraordinary power Bank On Yourself held, I felt very strongly that it would be unfair to others to keep it a secret. For the first time in my life, I began to feel the kind of burning passion to make a difference in the world that I'd heard other people describe.

> Once I knew from personal experience the extraordinary power of Bank On Yourself, I felt it would be unfair to keep it a secret, and it became my mission to educate others about it. But nothing could have prepared me for the firestorm of controversy that followed. . . .

It became my mission to educate the American public about Bank On Yourself, but nothing could have prepared me for the firestorm of controversy that followed.

Financial Secrets "They" Don't Want You to Know

As I mentioned, many people and entire industries are praying that you never discover this financial secret. In addition, the financial vehicle used for B.O.Y. is totally misunderstood and unfairly maligned by many so-called experts.

This book blasts apart those myths, misinformation, and misunderstandings, beyond any shadow of a doubt.

The tide has already begun to turn, and whenever I feel discouraged by criticism from people who are misinformed or who feel

threatened by B.O.Y., I open my bulging file cabinet full of unso-
licited letters from grateful folks who learned about B.O.Y. through
my Special Reports and newsletters. These letters tell how Bank On
Yourself has transformed their lives and helped them achieve many of
their short-term and long-term goals and dreams. One comment in
particular appears in almost every one: they say their only regret is
that they didn't find out about B.O.Y. sooner.

I'll introduce you to some of them in this book and let them describe their personal Bank On Yourself journeys in their own words. I
believe you'll find their stories as compelling as the facts and figures I
provide here.

B.O.Y. provides a proven long-term solution for the economic
challenges we all face today—one that doesn't depend on stock or real
estate investments that inevitably have those stomach-churning periods when the markets go down and down (which is exactly what's
happening as I write this). With a Bank On Yourself program, you can
leave those worries behind.

Proof that Conventional Financial and
Retirement Planning Isn't Working

It's become painfully clear that the conventional financial and retirement planning strategies we've been taught simply aren't working.
They were created to suit conditions that no longer exist. The percentage of Americans who are confident they'll be able to afford a
comfortable retirement has plunged to historic lows. And most retirees have discovered they must give up many things they once considered essential, just to get by.

Almost every issue of the AARP magazine has heartbreaking stories
of retirees who thought they were well off but are now suffering great
financial hardship. Tragically, the *majority* of retirees, according to a
May 2008 AARP report, are having difficulty paying for essential
items, such as food, gas, and medicines. Many have had to put off
filling prescriptions or take smaller doses than prescribed to make
costly medicines last longer, and see doctors and dentists only when
absolutely necessary, because their interest and investment income has
disappeared.

The same report revealed that "substantial numbers" of people over sixty-five are having to eat out less, postpone travel, and put off major purchases. This is on *top* of the pared-down lifestyle many are already living. (And that report came out *before* the financial meltdown that occurred in the fall of 2008.)

Do you think these folks worked hard all their lives so they could struggle to get by in retirement? I know that's not part of my plan, and I doubt it's part of yours.

And while most people plan to live on a lower income after they retire, many experts now predict retirees will actually need at least as much income as they had before retirement. One study released in July 2008 by Hewitt Associates, a human resources consulting company, found that, on average, people will need to replace *126 percent* of their pre-retirement income, when factoring in inflation, longer life spans, and skyrocketing medical costs.

Many pre-retirees have had to postpone retirement, and many retirees are being forced to go back to work at a time when older workers are finding it much harder to find jobs. What more proof do we need to know that conventional financial and retirement planning methods aren't working?

The Truth About Traditional Investment Strategies

As I write this in late 2008, the S&P 500 and the Dow are right back where they were ten long years earlier.

How many times during those years were your hopes raised, only to be dashed again and again?

Those losses don't even take into account inflation, which totaled more than 30 percent during that period. You could have gotten the same results putting your money under your mattress—but without all the nail-biting and sleepless nights!

Unfortunately, most Americans are digging themselves deeper into a financial hole every year, with no way of knowing how long it will take to crawl out.

As you'll discover in chapter 3, Wall Street's dirty little secret is that it's the norm, *not* the exception, for the stock market to end up going nowhere for very long periods of time.

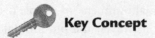 **Key Concept**

Here's a good question to ask yourself to determine how well your financial or retirement plan is working: do you know what your nest egg will be worth in ten, twenty, or thirty years, or when you're ready to use it? If your answer is no, then do you really have a financial plan?

If history repeats itself, the stock market could go nowhere for another decade or longer. We all hope that doesn't happen, of course, but if it did, how would that affect your financial security and plans for retirement?

The reality is that if your financial future depends on a roll of the dice, you don't have a financial plan.

Clearly the conventional wisdom about diversifying by using a mixture of stocks, mutual funds, and bonds needs to be examined by anyone who's tired of relying on hope and luck to achieve financial goals. This book explodes the myths about investing in the stock market that have been responsible for countless broken dreams of retirement.

Can You Rely on Your Home Equity to Help Fund Your Retirement?

Of course, for most Americans, their home is their largest asset, and many are counting on the equity in their home to help fund their retirement.

Once again, history provides a clue of what we can really expect. According to the extensively researched book *Irrational Exuberance* by Robert Shiller, *the long-term average increase in home values has been just 1 percent a year, adjusted for inflation,* even taking several periods of rapid appreciation into account. The May 15, 2006, issue of *Fortune* magazine echoed that statistic under the headline "Don't Bank On Your House to Fund Your Retirement," noting that it's "hardly enough to pay for two decades of sunset years on sun-filled decks."

> The long-term average increase in home
> values has been just 1 percent a year,
> adjusted for inflation. And housing
> prices can go nowhere for very long
> periods of time.

A revealing article in the *Wall Street Journal* (March 23, 2008) titled "Housing Prices Can Stall for a Long Stretch of Time" tells the real story most Americans don't have a clue about. The article points out that "the inflation-adjusted average price of an existing home peaked in 1979, didn't bottom out until 1984 and didn't return to the 1979 level until 1995. In other words . . . home prices went nowhere for 16 years."

Most people I've surveyed don't know or remember that. But once again, history does have a way of repeating itself, and a good question to ask yourself is how would your plans for retirement be affected if your home value went nowhere for sixteen years?

The Pension and Retirement Plan Crisis

Once upon a time, in the "good old days," when an employee gave a lifetime of service to "the company," the reward was traditionally a gold watch . . . and a pension benefit that would make his or her retirement years truly golden. Those days are long gone.

> According to Bloomberg board member
> (and journalist) Jane Bryant Quinn, writing
> in the *AARP Bulletin* (October 2007),
> "Retirement experts used to talk about
> finances as a three-legged stool: Social
> Security, pensions and personal savings.
> For one thing, the pension leg has
> collapsed entirely at many companies.
> And none of these legs can be taken
> for granted."

Most companies have moved away from pension plans, in which they provide their retirees with a set benefit each month, to such plans as 401(k)s, which put the burden of saving and investing for retirement squarely on the employees' shoulders—a responsibility most are totally unprepared for. Is it any wonder that many experts are now concluding that 401(k)s have been an abysmal failure?

And many companies that do sponsor 401(k) plans have drastically reduced or even eliminated the amount they match of their employees' contributions.

In addition, there are dangerous pitfalls to saving for retirement in 401(k) plans and IRAs that most people don't discover until it's too late, which I reveal in chapter 5.

Social Security and Medicare Are Going Belly Up

In March 2008, Treasury Secretary Henry Paulson warned that the country was facing a fiscal train wreck unless something was done about predicted Social Security and Medicare shortfalls. The Social Security trust fund is predicted to go bust in 2041. That's pretty scary when you consider that the majority of people over sixty-five rely on Social Security for at least half of their income, and 61 percent of pre-retirees age fifty and over are counting on it for their main source of income in retirement.

Government officials have repeatedly warned that the only way to fix this situation is through some combination of benefit cuts and tax increases.

The problem is even worse for Medicare, which will be exhausted by 2018 and *already* spends more than it collects.

Given all these factors, does it come as a surprise that many Americans are postponing retirement indefinitely? Americans' confidence in reaching an affordable retirement has plunged, with only 18 percent confident that it will happen for them, according to the 2008 Retirement Confidence Survey by the Employee Benefit Research Institute. Of those already retired, the survey revealed, only 29 percent are now confident of this.

Which explains why many retirees have been forced to go back to work. Like the seventy-seven-year-old subscriber to my newsletter, who wrote me that he wished he'd known about B.O.Y. years ago. He had to take a job climbing on roofs to install rain gutters to pay for medical expenses his health insurance didn't cover. Sadly, this scenario is playing out all too often across the country.

But it *doesn't* have to be that way!

A Plan You Can Count On

You don't have to accept risk, volatility, and unpredictability as givens. There *is* a proven and better way, revealed in the pages of this book. The letters I receive from people who use the Bank On Yourself method are compelling testaments to that, like the one I received from Mike LaPlante that read in part:

> After working for 25 years, I feel for the first time that my retire-ment is properly squared away. I no longer worry about where to put my money to chase a higher return. Bank On Yourself takes the gut feeling worry of, "Am I doing the right thing?" away, and allows me to focus on other more fun things in my life.
>
> Yes, I *do* wish I'd started earlier, but I suppose it took me this long to make enough of the financial mistakes I've made to allow B.O.Y. to reveal itself to me as the gem it really is.
>
> This is the best financial lesson I've ever been taught. I feel com-pletely at peace with my decision to move forward with this.

Growing a nest egg and a retirement income you can count on *doesn't* have to be a crapshoot. If you're tired of gambling with your financial future and are ready to start *knowing* how good it could be, read on. . . .

CHAPTER 2

How to Get Back Every Penny You Pay for Major Purchases

The greatest obstacle to discovering the shape of the earth, the continents, and the oceans was not ignorance—it was the illusion of knowledge.
—DANIEL BOORSTIN (1914–2004),
historian, Library of Congress

Is it really possible to "spend and grow wealthy"? Well, not if you're making major purchases the way most people do—by financing or leasing them, or even by paying cash for them. In fact, you may be shocked to learn how much wealth you are unnecessarily losing by buying things any of these conventional ways.

If you're scratching your head and wondering how in the world you could grow wealthy by buying the things you want and need, I'm about to reveal all the details of how this works. It will revolutionize the way you look at money and financing.

But please understand this is about a different way to pay for things—it's *not* about living above your means or keeping up with your neighbors.

When I talk about getting back what you pay for major purchases, some people get angry or insist I must be trying to pull the wool over their eyes. And I'll admit it may sound too good to be true, but it's something almost anyone can do, and at least 100,000 Americans I know of are already doing it. So please reserve your judgment until after you've heard me out.

Can you imagine being able to buy a brand-new car every few years and to get back every penny you paid for it, along with any interest charges you would have paid to banks and finance companies? What

17

if you could take that dream vacation with all the frills, but *without* feeling guilty, because you know you'll recover all the money you spent on it?

How would your life be different if you could have and enjoy the things you want—a state-of-the-art home theater or chef's kitchen, a boat or RV, a cottage at the beach or in the mountains, membership in an exclusive country club, business equipment, or any other big-ticket item you've been dreaming about—knowing you could do that without missing a single beat in growing a nest egg you can predict and count on?

Bank On Yourself offers a much better way to pay for cars and other major purchases that lets you get back all the money you pay for them. And not just the ticket price, but also all the interest you might have otherwise paid to a bank, finance or leasing company, or credit card. Perhaps best of all, using this method lets you grow your nest egg at the same time—predictably, so you don't lose any sleep over it.

In fact, many people could comfortably retire on the money they'd recapture *just* by paying for their cars and vacations the Bank On Yourself Spend and Grow Wealthy way. And they wouldn't have to endure the gut-wrenching ups and downs of the stock or real estate markets to do it. But you don't have to stop with getting back the cost of your cars and vacations, because the same principle applies to any major purchase you make.

Many people could comfortably retire on the money they'd recapture just by paying for their cars the Bank On Yourself Spend and Grow Wealthy way—without the risk of the stock and real estate markets.

To understand just how easy it is to Spend and Grow Wealthy, let's look at the most common way people finance a car—using bank or dealer financing.

Financing Big-Ticket Items Using Other People's Money

Let's say you decide to finance a $30,000 car loan over four years, through the ABC Finance Company. (Note: It doesn't really matter how much the car costs or how long you're going to keep it. I'm just using a $30,000, four-year car loan as an example.)

Okay, so you sign the paperwork, ABC Finance pays the dealership $30,000, and you drive the car off the lot.

Your monthly payments, figuring at an interest rate of 7.5 percent (a typical rate as I write this in mid-2008), will be $725. Over four years, that's a total of $34,800 you'll pay back on your loan.

When you make your last payment, you'll have a four-year-old car, worth whatever its trade-in value happens to be.

But who has your $34,800?

Yup, the ABC Finance Company has it.

Now let's say that you decide to trade that car in and borrow another $30,000 from ABC Finance for your next car.

Where did ABC Finance get the money they're going to lend you?

They got it from *you*, of course. And from other people like you who haven't discovered the Spend and Grow Wealthy way to buy things yet.

If you finance all your cars through ABC Finance for the next forty years, how much will it cost you?

In this example, that would be ten cars at $34,800, for a total of $348,000.

Do you see that all this money is going to go out of your pocket and into someone else's? The ABC Finance Company's pocket, the car dealership's pocket, and the car manufacturer's pocket. Everybody's making money on these transactions—*except you!*

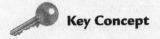 **Key Concept**

Far more money will leave your home just to buy cars over your lifetime than most people ever manage to save up for retirement. In fact, the median amount pre-retirees between the ages of fifty-five and sixty-four have saved up in their retirement plan is $88,000. Most people will spend several times that amount on their cars over their lifetime.

What if there was a way to enjoy those cars (and vacations, home remodels, and all your other major purchases) and get back every penny you paid for them to grow a nest egg that you can predict and count on? And what if that nest egg could keep right on growing, even when the stock and real estate markets are tanking?

It's not a pipe dream. And, as I mentioned, more than 100,000 Americans are already doing it—with Bank On Yourself.

So what the heck *is* Bank On Yourself, and how does it work?

Financing Big-Ticket Items the B.O.Y. Spend and Grow Wealthy Way

To understand the power of it, let's go back to our example of buying a car, except this time imagine you're buying the exact same car as in the previous scenario, but instead of borrowing $30,000 from a finance company, you're going to borrow it from your own Bank On Yourself plan.

I don't want you to get hung up on how you got the $30,000 into your plan, and keep in mind we could be using *any* number here and it would work just as well. (And later on, I'll show you several ways you may be able to start a B.O.Y. plan with money you already have.) For now, just follow along with this example, because it illustrates a mind-bending financial principle that's not taught in business, economics, or finance courses, and that most people have never even considered.

Okay, so you borrow the $30,000 from your Bank On Yourself plan and pay it directly to the dealership. You didn't have to fill out a credit application, because it's your money. You drive your new car off the lot. You own it and get the title to it right away.

About thirty days later, your first payment is due, but now you write the check to your own Bank On Yourself plan—a pool of money you own and control—instead of to a finance company.

And let's say you decide to pay the loan back at the exact same rate as you would have paid to ABC Finance—$725 a month for four years.

Your total payments are the same—$34,800. But when the loan is paid off, you have the car, *and* all the money you paid for it is right back in your Bank On Yourself plan. In fact, there's *more* than the $34,800 in your plan, because, incredibly, your plan has been earning money for you during the *entire* four years on *every* single penny of the $30,000 you borrowed from it!

> When the loan is paid off, you have the car
> *and* all the money you paid for it right back
> in your Bank On Yourself plan, and *then*
> some, because your plan has been earning
> money for you the *entire* time on every
> single penny you borrowed from it!

So, in this scenario, you recaptured the full cost of your car, along with the interest that would have gone to an outside finance company, plus some extra profit. You ended up with the car *and* all the money you paid for the car!

And now you can recycle those dollars over and over again to buy all your future cars the same way. The bottom line is that if you bought those same ten $30,000 cars over that same forty-year period using your B.O.Y. plan, you could have the $348,000 the finance company, car dealership, and manufacturer would have made off of you . . . and *then* some!

You could use this same process to get back the money you'd pay for *any* major purchase, including vacations, home improvements, a boat or an RV, a home theater, country club initiation fees, business equipment, a second home in the mountains or at the beach, a college education, or anything else your heart desires.

 Key Concept

This is all happening simply because your money is going from one of your pockets into another one of your pockets—your Bank On Yourself plan—instead of going into someone *else's* pocket. The difference is that in this case, you're both the consumer *and* the source of financing.

This is what happens when you cut out the middleman (the bank or finance company). And the difference it can make in how much wealth you end up with will astonish you, as you'll soon discover.

It's not rocket science, but most of us have never been taught this powerful principle of finance that turns the direction of financial energy in our lives from cash *out* to cash *in*.

Of course, you may prefer to lease your cars, because the monthly payments can be lower than if you financed the car. But not only do you have *nothing* to show for your money at the end of a lease, not even a trade-in, you will still be out every penny you paid to the leasing company.

How Using a Savings or Money Market Account Compares to B.O.Y.

Maybe you're thinking you can get a result similar to Bank On Yourself by using a savings or money market account or CD, or perhaps by borrowing the money from your 401(k). But can you really? Let's see . . .

Let's say you save up money in one of those traditional ways, planning to pay cash for a major purchase. The day comes when you hit your savings goal and pull out all your money to buy that car or go on that vacation. How much interest are you now going to earn on that money?

Zero, right? And if you were to make payments back into that savings account or whatever, your principal would build back up slowly. You'd be receiving *very* small amounts of interest for many months or years, until you had paid in enough for the principal to build up substantially.

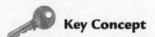 **Key Concept**

Conventional wisdom tells us that paying cash is a better solution than financing or leasing things, but the reality is that you finance *everything* you buy. Why? Because you either *pay* interest to someone else to use their money, or you *give up* the interest or investment income you *could* have earned on your money, had you invested it instead of paying cash.

This seems obvious when you think about it, but somehow, until it's called to our attention, most of us don't realize this fact.

Figure 1 shows what happens when you use a savings or money market account to make major purchases.

Your Dollar Target

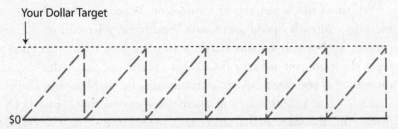

Figure 1—Balance in a savings account that is used periodically for major purchases

As you can see, every time you accumulate enough in this account to hit your dollar target, whether that's $3,000, $30,000, or $300,000, then pull it out to make your purchase, you're left with *nothing* to earn interest on.

If you were trying to take retirement income from this account, how long do you think it would last?

Now let's compare that with accumulating or saving money in a Bank On Yourself plan. There are some costs involved with a B.O.Y. plan—after all, you're getting many advantages and guarantees that you *don't* get with a savings, money market, or investment account. That's why you'll typically reach the point where you hit your dollar target and have enough to buy a car—or anything else you want—more quickly in a savings account than you would in a B.O.Y. plan . . . but *only* early on. After that, the B.O.Y. plan ramps up and leaves other financial vehicles and methods in the dust, as you can see in Figure 2.

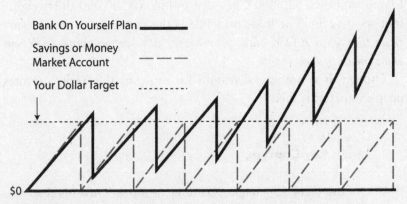

Figure 2—Comparison of growth in B.O.Y. versus savings account

No, that's not a mistake or a misprint. When you buy things the Bank On Yourself Spend and Grow Wealthy way I reveal in the next part of this book, it actually makes your plan grow over time. Surprisingly, the more you use your B.O.Y. plan to finance things this way, the more money you could have to use and enjoy throughout your lifetime.

And, while it will take you a little longer—at first—in a B.O.Y. plan to hit the same dollar target as it would in a savings account, it may help to think of it as a start-up phase, just as you'd have if you were starting up a new business—what we might call the I Finance Myself Company. This start-up is a one-time phase that pays a *lifetime* of benefits, because a B.O.Y. plan is designed to grow more efficiently every year you have it.

For reasons I'll explain later, you won't borrow 100 percent of your equity in a B.O.Y. plan, which is why the second chart shows that you hold off a little while longer after the B.O.Y. plan has reached the dollar goal the first time, before you take out your dollar target.

Perhaps you're wondering why I didn't include any numbers on the chart comparing B.O.Y. to a savings account. One reason is that no two B.O.Y. plans are alike. Every plan is custom-designed to fit a person's unique situation, goals, and dreams. And a number of factors come into play. So how much you'll have in your plan at any given point will be unique to your plan.

The second reason I didn't include specific numbers is that it doesn't matter what your dollar goal is or whether you want to use the money in your plan to take a $3,000 vacation in the Caribbean Islands, to buy a $30,000 Chevy, or to buy a $300,000 thirty-eight-foot sport yacht. The basic principle is the same: *if you run the purchase through a B.O.Y. plan, your money can keep growing while you enjoy the things you want!*

Though there are several reasons for this, one that really captures people's interest is this:

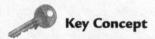 **Key Concept**

One of the seemingly magical features of a B.O.Y. plan is that if you borrow $3,000 or $30,000 or even $300,000 from your plan to buy something or to invest elsewhere, *all* the money you borrowed continues earning for you in your plan at the exact same pace, as though you never touched a dime of it! I'll explain soon exactly how that's possible.

After comparing the options of using a savings or money market account versus a B.O.Y. plan to pay for big-ticket items, is there any question in your mind which of these two results you'd rather have?

Here's something else to consider: you'll typically pay income taxes on the growth you get in a regular savings account. However, in the next part of this book, I'll explain how under current tax laws it's possible to get your hands on the growth you receive in a B.O.Y. plan without owing taxes on it.

Now let's see what would happen if you borrowed the money from your 401(k) or other retirement plan to pay cash for your major purchases.

Using a 401(k) or Other Retirement Plan to Finance Major Purchases

Some government-sponsored plans do allow you to borrow part of your money. But if you do it that way, you'll have to sell your assets and investments and give up the interest or investment income you could have made on that money.

You don't have to sell or liquidate anything or give up a penny of growth when you use your equity in a Bank On Yourself plan.

Of course, if you're trying to save up money in any kind of investment or brokerage account to pay cash for a major purchase, the biggest question is going to be: *will the money even be there when you plan or hope to use it?*

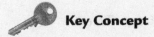 **Key Concept**

Your retirement plan investments are typically subject to market risk and volatility. However, your principal in a B.O.Y. plan won't vanish due to a stock or real estate market correction. And your growth, as soon as it's credited to your plan, is locked in.

Also, many people do not realize how many rules and restrictions come with government-sponsored plans like 401(k)s. For example, do you know what happens if you take a loan and then lose or leave your job?

With few exceptions, the loan must be paid back in *full* in sixty days, or you'll have to pay taxes and "premature distribution" penalties on the entire unpaid loan amount.

 Key Concept

When you borrow from a Bank On Yourself plan, *you* set your loan repayment schedule. You can reduce or even skip some payments, if you had to, and no one's going to hassle you, charge you late fees, send a goon squad after you to repossess your stuff, or foreclose on your home.

The Bank On Yourself program works through a proven financial product that's existed for over a hundred years, but with a unique twist, which I'll tell you all about in the next section of this book.

If you're wondering where you'll get the money to fund a B.O.Y. plan, I'll cover that, too—and you may be surprised at how often people are able to do this without having to come up with a lot of extra money out of pocket. For now, I just want you to see the incredible value in using this method to finance your large purchases.

As you'll see, the difference that running your major purchases through a B.O.Y. plan, instead of using traditional financing or paying cash, can be staggering over the course of your lifetime.

* * *

How Bank On Yourself Makes Dreams Come True

Alice Englund, who has been using Bank On Yourself for four years, perfectly captured the power of this method in the following description of her experience (which I've included here with her permission):

Bank On Yourself has definitely been working for me. Next month I'm taking my dream vacation to Kauai, Hawaii, for two full weeks. I'm staying in a beautiful hotel right on the beach and doing all the fun things I wouldn't have been able to afford if it wasn't for my Bank On Yourself plan.

The best part is, I'm getting back the cost of this fabulous vacation —that's what happens when you Bank On Yourself. And I added on every extra activity I wanted, from a helicopter ride and a sunset dinner sail, to zipping through the jungle, biking down a canyon, and kayaking up a river, plus two Hawaiian-style massages and a luau, complete with a hula show.

If I'd saved up the money for this vacation in a savings or money market account, I'd have felt guilty spending it. And I'd have worried that if I spent this much on a "luxury," I wouldn't have the money if an emergency came up and I needed it to keep my head above water.

But since I discovered B.O.Y., I'm simply borrowing the money for the trip from my plan—not creating debt on a credit card, like I used to. This way I can pay cash for the trip and then pay my plan back, instead of flushing the money down the drain to a credit card company.

In a fairly short period of time, the money will be completely paid back, and my plan will be ready to use again to fund my next "life-improvement project" or exciting adventure.

Not only that, the interest I used to pay to the credit card companies now lands right back in my own Bank On Yourself plan, along with the full cost of the trip or project, because I paid for it in this way.

So, in the end, the trip really isn't costing me a dime. In fact, I'm *making* money on it! And now that I've laid the groundwork, I'll be able to take fabulous vacations every two years for the rest of my life.

In the four years since I started my Bank On Yourself plan, I've also used it to finance two life-improvement projects.

First, I installed a privacy fence, built a patio, and landscaped my yard with flowering bushes. Then last Christmas I visited my daughter and her family back East and bought them the computer she and my grandkids needed for school. And I've already recovered the entire cost of both of those purchases.

One of the *most* important reasons I love Bank On Yourself is that *I no longer have to worry about whether I'll be able to reach my retirement goals. B.O.Y. lets me do that without worrying about what's happening in my 401(k) or what my house is worth.*

That gives me the peace of mind I never had before I had my "money-multiplying" Bank On Yourself plan.

Some of my friends and family thought I was into one of those get-rich-quick money schemes when I first told them I was starting a B.O.Y. plan. But now that they can see all the incredible benefits I'm getting, and how relaxed and happy I am about money, they're all starting to come around and ask me how they can start plans of their own. They tell me they wish they'd listened to me sooner when I tried to tell them about this.

So what is the financial vehicle that can allow you to accomplish this? Keep reading, because I'm about to reveal the surprising secret that could make all this—and more—possible for you.

PART TWO

Katie and Paul

CHAPTER 3

The Adventure Begins

All truth goes through three stages: It is ridiculed;
then it is radically opposed; and only much later
will it be accepted as self-evident.

—ARTHUR SCHOPENHAUER, philosopher

What's the process of getting started with a Bank On Yourself plan? The
details are revealed in Paul and Katie's story, which is based on the experi-
ences of real people (all projections are based on the 2008 rates, assump-
tions, and tax laws, which are subject to change) . . .

Paul Harper wasn't having a good day.

He had promised himself that he wouldn't look at the stock market
numbers any more. Mid-morning he happened to notice, without
meaning to, that the Dow was up 35 points. As five o'clock rolled
around, he couldn't resist checking to see if the gain had held.

More bad news. The Dow had closed down 116 points. That
meant his 401(k) plan, battered for months, must have taken another
beating. Now he couldn't resist knowing the rest of the story, how
badly he had been hurt. He clicked on the online bookmark for his
plan balance.

When his account information filled the screen, he shook his head
in disgust. Just since the first of the month, the value of his plan was
down more than $3,500, on top of the previous month's heart-
stopping decline. He gazed out the window, too distracted to notice
the handsome view of snow-capped peaks visible from his office in the
Denver suburb of Aurora.

"Hey, you look like you just got some really bad news." Paul recognized the voice of Rob Martinez, his ride home for the day.

"You got that right," Paul said, groaning and rolling his eyes. "My
401(k) is killing me."

"Right now, the word '401(k)' is banned in my house."

"I promise myself I won't look, but then I do, and my heartburn kicks right in."

"Hey—everybody has their own way of coping with things. I guess pretending it's not happening works as well as anything else," Rob said.

Paul shot Rob a rueful smile. "Katie and I are both forty years old, so I know we have some time left to put together enough to retire on. But when you watch your retirement fund shrinking instead of growing, you wonder. I keep thinking, are we all going to end up like my parents?"

Looking out the window so Rob wouldn't see how upset he really was, Paul continued, "They're hardly able to afford eating out, they wear their coats around the house to keep the heating bills down, and think they're lucky because they haven't had to sell the house, like some of their friends have. We told them they could move in with us, of course, if it came to that. But my dad keeps insisting he'd never want to be a burden to us."

"Yeah, I know. It hasn't turned out the way my folks thought it would, either," Rob sympathized. "A couple years ago, they bought a motor home and had planned to spend the winters traveling through Arizona and California. That was the dream that kept them going for *years* before they retired. They planned out every detail. They were able to do it for one year and then their interest and investment income dried up. They had to sell their motor home and resign themselves to the long winters here. My mom's got arthritis and the cold just kills her."

Paul shrugged into his coat and, as the two of them started down the hall toward the parking lot, he said, "Some days I wonder if I should just dump all my stocks and mutual funds and put everything in a money market account. But I'm not sure that's the answer, either . . ."

"Have you ever heard of Bank On Yourself?" Rob asked.

"No. What is it?"

"It's a way to get back the money you spend on major purchases, along with the interest you're paying," Rob explained. "Instead of writing checks to banks, credit cards, and finance companies, you basically write the checks to yourself—to your own Bank On Yourself plan."

Rob went on, "All that money builds up in your plan over the years, and you can use it as a retirement fund. But it's not like putting the money into the stock market, or investing in real estate. The value of the plan doesn't bounce around like they do."

Paul's eyes narrowed. "Rob, what have you been smoking?" he asked.

"Hey, I know! I was skeptical at first, too, but the more I looked into it and compared it to other options, the more sense it made."

"Well, you know what they say—if it sounds too good to be true, it probably is. And this sounds way too good to be true," Paul said, clearly becoming impatient with Rob.

"No kidding," Rob agreed. By this time they had reached Rob's SUV. He started the engine and turned up the heater, and then fetched a scraper to clear the ice off the windshield. Rob continued, "But B.O.Y. isn't a get-rich-quick scheme. It doesn't happen overnight."

"The value keeps going up even when the market is down? Is that what you're saying?"

"When you Bank On Yourself, if the market tanks, both your principal and growth are locked in. You don't go backward. In fact, you get a guaranteed increase *every* year."

Rob answered, "I don't blame you for that suspicious look on your face. But that's right—even if the market tanks, both your principal and growth are locked in. You don't go backward. In fact, you get a guaranteed increase every year."

"So what is it—some kind of savings or investment account?"

"It's not an investment, which is great, because I might be sweating bullets if it was. I'm like you," Rob said. "There's been a lot of times I've dreaded checking the balance in my 401(k). But I always look forward to opening my B.O.Y. statement. It's always good news. With B.O.Y., I don't have to worry anymore about what to invest in or where to get a higher rate of return. It's why I don't sweat it even when my 401(k) takes a hit."

"That would be nice, for a change," Paul said as they both got into the car and Rob steered out of the parking lot. "But that part about getting back the cost of major purchases, and the interest, too—I don't see how that's possible."

"That's what I thought at first. But as I said, I did my homework. And now I can't deny that it's for real, because in a few months I'll have gotten back every penny I paid for this car. And from then on I'll be able to use those same dollars over and over again to buy a new car every four years or so."

Because Paul and Rob worked in different parts of the company and had car-pooled only a few times before, Paul was beginning to wonder if Rob was telling this straight. Somehow it sounded too far-fetched. He got even more doubtful with Rob's next statement: "I already know how much money I'll have in the plan at retirement, and how much income I'll be able to count on taking each year."

Rob went on, "And unless they change the tax laws, I won't have to pay taxes on the income I take from the plan. It's not like a 401(k), where you cross your fingers and hope you'll have enough to retire on, and then you have to pay taxes on every dollar you take out."

Then he made a claim that left Paul even more uncertain. "One of the things that fascinated me about Bank On Yourself is that after I borrowed $35,000 from my B.O.Y. plan so I could pay cash for this SUV, my plan kept right on growing as though all that money was still in it!"

Paul studied Rob for a long moment. Then he said, "Okay, Rob, I get it. You're jerking my chain, right? You're either having fun with me, making it all up, or else somebody's sold you a bill of goods."

Rob laughed out loud, such a full-body laugh that Paul was sure it was a confession that Rob had just been teasing him or testing him with an outrageous tale. Playing along, Paul smiled, waiting for the confession. He got a surprise instead.

"I've shared my Bank On Yourself experiences with quite a few people," Rob said. "Most of them are doubtful when they first hear about it, but this is the first time anybody's accused me of making it up!"

"Well, if it's not an investment and it's something that grows in a secure way, what the heck is it?"

"I want to tell you what it is, but I'm afraid you'll have the same knee-jerk reaction a lot of people do, because they've been totally misinformed about it. If they really knew the facts, and how it works, they'd be tripping over themselves to do it."

> "I want to tell you what Bank On Yourself is, but I'm afraid you'll have the same reaction a lot of people do, because they've been misinformed about it. If people knew the facts, they'd trip over themselves to do it."

He went on, "I'll tell you what. I'll introduce you to Jack Richards, the man who helped me set up my plan. He's a Bank On Yourself Authorized Advisor. If you meet with him and don't come away convinced that what I've been telling you is absolutely true, and don't want to start your own plan, I'll pay for you and your wife to go out to dinner once a week for a month. If I'm lyin', I'm buyin'."

"*Any* restaurant we want?"

"Any restaurant you want," Rob agreed.

"I need to tell you," Paul said, "that my wife, Katie, is a gourmet cook. She's always wanting to go out to dinner at the most expensive restaurants and I'm always telling her those places aren't in our budget." Saying it almost like a threat, Paul announced, "This is gonna *cost* you."

"No, it's not," Rob said confidently. "I'm not a gambling man. You're going to sit down with Jack Richards, and then you'll come and tell me the two of you have decided to sign up for a plan of your own."

"You've got a deal! But the *only* reason I'm doing it is that I want those free dinners," Paul said.

"You won't regret it. Listen to this: they have this deal where you can go to a Web site and take the Bank On Yourself Challenge, where they'll pay a big cash reward to the first person who can show they use any other financial strategy or product that gives them the advantages and guarantees that B.O.Y. does. As far as I know, no one's been able to beat that challenge."

> "There's a big cash reward being offered
> to the first person who can show they
> use any other financial strategy that gives
> them the advantages and guarantees that
> Bank On Yourself does. You can take the
> Bank On Yourself Challenge and get
> a summary of how B.O.Y. works
> at www.BankOnYourself.com."

"And if I wanted to take the challenge, I would . . .?"

"You'd go online to **www.BankOnYourself.com**. You can get a free report there, too, that summarizes how Bank On Yourself works. You and Katie should read it before you see Jack."

Paul said, "I'm writing that down right now."

"Now . . . do I have your word you're really going to see Jack and listen to what he has to say?"

"Wait a minute," Paul said. "How much will it cost me to meet with Jack?"

"It won't cost you anything to meet with him, and he won't let you buy anything at your first meeting, either. First he'll do an analysis for you and Katie that will show you how much your financial picture could improve if you started a plan customized for your situation. It'll show you how much more money you could have by running your major purchases through a Bank On Yourself plan, and how much retirement income you could have as a result, *after* taking fees and costs into account, so you don't have any surprises," Rob assured him.

Paul looked relieved. "Good. I'm pretty tired of the surprises I've been getting in my 401(k) . . ."

"Then you're going to *love* Bank On Yourself. The only surprises I've gotten from my B.O.Y. plan are good ones!" Rob said. "What I'm excited about is that in a few months, I'll have gotten back all the money I paid for this SUV, plus the interest the finance company used to make off me. Then I'm gonna take that money and march into the dealership—with cash in hand—and finance my next new car using the money I got back by paying for this car the B.O.Y. way. So, are you going to take me up on the bet and promise you'll talk to Jack?"

"All right, already. I promise! Now will you tell me what it is, or is this some kind of secret that if you told me, you'd have to kill me?"

Rob let out a roar of laughter. "You've got one vivid imagination, Paul. No, it's nothing like that."

"So why do you need a promise from me?"

"You'll understand when I tell you."

Paul looked at him suspiciously and finally said, "Okay, you've got my word. What's the mystery?"

"No mystery," Rob said. "It's just that this is based on a financial tool that most people don't understand and they get turned off and won't even listen to the whole story."

"And that financial tool is . . . ?"

"Life insurance."

"*Life insurance?*" Paul asked, incredulous.

"Yeah, but it's a special kind of life insurance that some rich people have known about for a long time but most people—and even most financial experts—have never heard of. And my plan is through one of the financially strongest life insurance groups in the world."

"It's a special kind of life insurance policy that some wealthy people have known about for a long time but most people— and even most financial experts—have never heard of."

"Insurance," Paul repeated, as though he still couldn't believe what he'd heard. "You're telling me this guy is going to sell me a life insurance policy that will make me wealthy. Is that what you're saying?"

"What I'm telling you is that you've agreed to sit down with my advisor and not make up your mind until you've given him a chance to explain this all the way through. That's our deal, right?"

Not sounding very confident about what he had let himself in for, Paul answered by sticking out his hand. Reluctantly. Rob understood the gesture. He took Paul's hand and shook it once. They had a deal.

* * *

The following week, Paul and his wife, Katie, met with Rob's Bank On Yourself Advisor, Jack Richards. Katie was momentarily annoyed with herself; she had somehow expected a financial advisor to be an anemic person with a washed-out look and now realized what a cliché image that was, as she took in Jack's athletic build and broad shoulders, and what she saw as a stern look contradicted by friendly eyes.

Glancing around the office, Paul and Katie couldn't help but notice that almost every inch of wall space was covered with photos of people. Not rock stars, or famous faces from the movies or TV, or politicians. They looked like everyday people.

Jack saw the looks on their faces and explained that a few years earlier, he had started asking his clients to send him pictures of themselves with the things they had bought or done using their B.O.Y. plans. "At first they trickled in, but now I get new photos in the mail and by e-mail all the time. I don't have enough wall space anymore to put 'em all up," he said, adding, "I've been doing this for a while."

Paul and Katie joined him for a closer look. Katie noticed that some of the photos were signed and had notes of thanks written on them, but then her attention was distracted as the glass from one of the frames gave a mirror-like reflection of herself and her husband. She had always liked the way they looked together, his 5' 11" just the right height above her five-inches-shorter stature, his black, curly hair and intense eyes a contrast to her own blond hair, wide-set eyes, and narrow, still girlish face.

She pulled her attention back to the conversation. Jack was waving a hand at the collection of photos as he said, "What's amazing about B.O.Y. is how many different things people use it for." He started pointing at some of the photos. "This is Tim and Debbie with the RV that B.O.Y. bought. Here's Julie in her remodeled kitchen, and over here's the Campbell family collage—they've used their plan to buy five family cars now, and three trucks Bob uses in his business."

One photo was of a young man standing next to a campus student-services building. A note at the bottom said, "To Jack, with thanks for showing us how to get back the cost of Jason's tuition so we can use it for our retirement! —Bill and Carrie." Other pictures showed people with everything from a new air conditioner to a swimming pool, on a ski vacation in Switzerland, and even one taken at a wedding for one couple's daughter.

Jack said, "My clients don't pay for these things on credit cards or by taking a loan from a bank or finance company. With Bank On Yourself, they borrow the money out of their plan and then pay their plans back, along with the interest they previously paid to finance institutions. The people in these pictures are acting as their own source of financing. Which means they can get back the cost of major purchases and pocket some of the profits banks and finance companies used to make on them. And with B.O.Y., they can know what their financial future is going to be."

"When you become your own source of
financing using B.O.Y., you can get back the
cost of major purchases, along with the
interest you previously paid to finance
institutions. And you can know what your
financial future is going to be."

At that point, he caught the couple off guard with an unexpected question. "Do the two of you talk about dream places to go on vacation?"

"Not really," Paul said.

Katie shook her head, a faint sad smile on her lips. "Don't you know how much I want to travel to all those places I get gourmet recipes from?" and then, with a little shrug, she said to Jack, "He pretends to listen, but most of the time he doesn't hear a word I say."

Paul didn't let the complaint bother him. "She tries to talk to me when I'm watching a Broncos game. I keep telling her, 'Unless the house is on fire, save it till the game is over.'" To Katie he said, "You tell *me* which one of us doesn't listen." Jack was afraid this might dissolve into a family squabble, but then Paul and Katie looked at each other and started laughing. Obviously an old dispute that both of them had grown comfortable with.

Jack said, "So if you wanted to use your plan for travel, where would you go first?"

Katie didn't even have to stop and think. "*Paris!*" Her mouth turned down in a little frown and she went on without a pause, "But Europe is so expensive. Between covering our monthly bills and trying to save for retirement, we barely have enough money left to afford a ski weekend at a local slope twice a year, let alone Paris. I already feel guilty enough taking the vacations we do now, knowing we'll have those credit card bills to pay off."

Paul agreed. "Yeah, a trip to Paris would probably take twenty years of saving. Well, ten, anyway." He looked at Jack. "Right?"

Jack grinned as he got up out of his chair. "Every plan I design is tailored to the client's situation. No two are exactly alike." On the wall, he pointed to a picture of a couple standing at the base of the Eiffel Tower. "Paula and Bill went on a two-week European tour about four years into their plan." Then he pointed to another. "This is Mike and Christina," he said. "They made a Paris trip the first thing they used their plan for. It took them only two years from the day they started."

Jack continued, "But listen to this: Mike and Christina got back the money they paid for that trip in just two years and then used those dollars for a cruise of the Greek Islands. Do you get the point?" he asked. "Please don't get me wrong. I'm *not* encouraging you to live beyond your means. That's *not* what B.O.Y. is about. But when you finance purchases like these through a Bank On Yourself plan, you *don't* have to choose between enjoying things today and saving for tomorrow. You can do both at the same time."

"When you finance purchases through a B.O.Y. plan, you *don't* have to choose between enjoying things today and saving for tomorrow. You can do both at the same time."

Katie got up to take a closer look. It was one of those incredible photos, the kind that people treasure forever. They were looking at each other instead of at the camera. "You can just see their joy and their love," she said. "It's written all over their faces plain as day." Paul joined her. What struck him most was that the couple looked hardly thirty years old.

"So," Jack said, "it looks like I should be putting down 'travel' as one of your goals. Yes?"

"Yes," they both answered as if with one voice, then looked at each other and smiled.

"Let me tell you a few things about what Bank On Yourself can make happen for you," Jack said. As he wrote a note on his pad, he explained, "A B.O.Y. plan comes with some pretty extraordinary advantages, and one is that you're in control of the equity in your plan. What I mean is, you can use the money however you want." Katie and Paul both nodded. He went on, "But listen to this: when you use the money to go on a trip, or pay for some home improvements or whatever . . . the money you borrowed continues to grow in value just as if you hadn't taken it out."

Paul remembered how skeptical he had been when Rob had made the same claim. "How's that possible?" he asked Jack.

"It's a provision built into the plan. Well, okay," he corrected. "Not many insurance companies have policies with that feature. But if you decide to do this, I'll use a company to administer your plan that does have it."

Katie's eyes widened as she said, "That's incredible, being able to actually use the money in our plan and have it still be earning money for us! To be honest, it really *does* sound too good to be true."

"I know," Jack replied. "It did to me, too, at first. You'll come to see how it works as we get into the details."

Jack then explained that what he typically did first when a new client came in to see him was to prepare a Bank On Yourself Analysis to find out their short-term and long-term goals and dreams, and to get a snapshot of their current financial situation.

He told the couple, "Then I can go to work for you preparing a Bank On Yourself plan tailored to your unique situation. I'll design it to help you achieve as many of your goals as possible."

Picking up his writing pad, Jack came out from behind his desk to take a seat nearer the couple. "If it's okay with you," he said, "I'd like to start by finding out what your biggest financial concerns are. So—what keeps you up at night? Do you have any one big overriding financial concern?"

Katie said, "We both worry about what we'd do if one of us had an accident or a big medical problem. Or got fired or laid off. We don't have much of a cash reserve we could use in an emergency."

"It's not just us," Paul added. "Most of our friends are in the same boat—only a couple paychecks away from disaster. Sure, we could live off our credit cards for a while, but then we'd have all that stress knowing we've got to pay them back."

"We keep hearing you should have enough savings to cover your living expenses for six months or so," Katie said. "Good luck. I know we'd sleep a lot better if we had that, but we don't."

Jack scribbled on his pad and said, "I'll put 'emergency fund' down as your top short-term goal."

Paul said, "Rob told me he bought his SUV with money from his plan, and because he makes the payments and interest charges back to his plan, he gets back what he paid for it. What's that really about?"

"With a B.O.Y. plan, you could be doing that too. Are you going to be buying a new car soon?"

"I bought a Cadillac Executive Series earlier this year," Paul replied.

"Nice wheels," Jack said.

"I head up a product development team for Midas Solutions. We're a software company that develops specialized applications for banks. I think bankers trust you more if you look like you're doing well. With all the options I wanted, the price tag came to nearly $40,000."

"Financed, or leased?" Jack asked.

"I got around $10,000 for my trade-in and financed the other $30,000 through the dealership."

"And how often do you typically buy a new car?" Jack continued.

"When the warranty is running out," Paul said. "Usually every four years."

Jack went to his desk, tapped on his keyboard a few moments, then returned to his seat. He asked Paul, "So you borrowed $30,000, and car loan interest rates are running about 7.5 percent right now. Want to take a guess how much money you're going to pay in interest on that loan over the next four years?"

Paul thought for a second and said, "I suppose it's gotta be at least a couple thousand dollars."

Jack shook his head. "Closer to $5,000. And that's money you're never going to see again."

Paul whistled, as Katie said, "Wait a minute—that doesn't figure. If the interest rate is 7.5 percent, then the dollar amount of interest should be 7.5 percent of $30,000. That's something like $2,000, not $5,000."

"People sometimes think that, at first. But you're missing something," Jack said and then gave her a moment to figure it out.

"Oh," she said a little sheepishly. "It's that much every year . . . for four years."

"Yeah," Paul said. "I get it. But it's not 7.5 percent of $30,000 every year, because you're paying down the loan every month."

"Exactly," Jack answered. "The point is that you're paying something like $5,000 in interest over the life of the loan. So *some*body's getting rich on that deal, but it's definitely not you. How much money do you think will drain out of your pockets if you finance $30,000 every four years for your next ten cars—assuming the interest rate stays at 7.5 percent?"

Katie spoke up. "$30,000 times ten is $300,000, plus $5,000 interest times ten cars is $50,000. So it's going to be $350,000—that's an easy one."

"You nailed it," Jack said. "So while paying interest charges to an outside finance company is dangerous enough to your financial health, it's chump change compared to the total amount of money you're out when you finance things the way you've been doing."

He leaned forward to be sure he had their attention. "Wouldn't you rather have that $350,000 as extra money in your retirement fund? That's a big chunk of change that will help you be able to travel and enjoy your hobbies and interests when you retire. Would you sleep better at night if you knew you'd have that much more money?"

"If you finance ten $30,000 cars over your
lifetime through a finance company,
including the interest you'll pay and never
see again, you'll be out $350,000.
Wouldn't you rather have that extra
$350,000 to enrich your retirement?
Especially if you don't have to gamble your
hard-earned money by making riskier
investments to do it?"

Both Katie and Paul agreed that they would. Paul added, "And we won't even have to give up taking dream vacations or having a new car every four years to do it, if I'm understanding how this works?"

Jack smiled. "That's right, and that's why we call it the Spend and Grow Wealthy way to buy things. And the more you use your plan to finance things this way, and the longer you do it, the more money you could have. Without gambling with your hard-earned money by making riskier investments in order to chase higher rates of return. Sound good so far?"

"Yeah, it sounds good. Maybe even too good. I've just heard that life insurance isn't a good place to put your money. I know Rob says B.O.Y. doesn't use the kind of life insurance policy people are talking about when they say that, but you gotta admit that what you're saying sounds like magic. You know, if it wasn't for the bet Rob made with me, we might not even be sitting here," Paul said.

Jack seemed a little surprised and asked, "What bet?"

After Paul had fessed up, Jack laughed. He could already tell he was going to enjoy working with these two. "Sounds to me like you really didn't have a whole lot to lose by coming here today— you're either going to find out how you can get back the cost of your major purchases and use that money to fund your retirement, or you're going to get free dinners at great restaurants once a week for a month."

"Maybe so," said Paul, "but we're not letting you off easy. You're gonna have to prove this is everything you and Rob say it is.

"I love a challenge," Jack replied. "I'll show you why there's no other financial product or strategy that can give you all the advantages and guarantees of Bank On Yourself. And I'll *prove* to you that most experts don't even *know* about the kind of life insurance policy we use for B.O.Y. This is all going to make a lot more sense when I have enough information to custom-tailor a B.O.Y. plan that's just right for your particular situation. So can you help me understand more about your goals and dreams? What else comes to mind?"

"I can give you a long-term dream of mine," Katie said. "One of these years, I'd love to be able to take a month off and do volunteer work with the Children's Project in Ghana that our church runs."

Paul looked at his wife. "Load up the freezer with four weeks of your gourmet cooking before you leave, okay?" Turning to Jack, Paul explained, "It's really important to her. And I'd love if we could make it happen. But . . ." He ended with one of those resigned shrugs that means "no way in *this* lifetime."

Jack gestured at his photo-lined walls. "I've learned never to say 'never' to any of my clients' dreams." He went on, "But what about your goals for your retirement?"

Paul began hesitantly. "That's a big worry. A big question mark. The stock market has been so crazy. I've been having a recurring nightmare that I'll be saying that line that's been going around, 'Would you like fries with your order?' until the day I drop."

Katie managed a smile, but it was quickly replaced by sadness as she added, "My dad always said he thought he and my mom were in pretty good shape financially, but after the market crashed in 2000, he had to go back to work. In his seventies! Here we are in the middle of 2008, and it's replay time in the market."

"We wish we could afford to help him out," Paul said. "It's frustrating because it just seems like there's no way for most of us to really know for sure how much we'll have to retire on."

"I think," Jack told them, "that the American public has been sucked into believing that building a nest egg and a comfortable lifestyle in retirement means you have to accept risk, volatility, and unpredictability. We're told that over time we should be able to get the same kind of returns as the overall stock market. That's a myth. And it's probably been responsible for more broken retirement dreams than anything else."

"Oh, we know that one real well," Paul said, groaning, and Katie explained, "We both have 401(k) plans and that's pretty much all we've got put away for retirement. It kills us to see the money we worked so hard for disappear out of our 401(k)s into thin air. I almost cried when I saw how much we'd lost last month alone. And it's all out of our control, anyway."

Paul, a relocated New Yorker, had a way of talking fast when he was upset. His words came out in a stream. "We keep hearing that investing is a long-term strategy, if you stick with it you'll do okay in the long run, but when your numbers are lower at the end of the year than the year before, and the market is right back where it was ten years ago, that 'long-term' business doesn't wash. It's just incredibly scary. And how do you look your wife in the eye and say, 'Everything's gonna be just fine, sweetie,' when you feel in your heart it's a lie." He reached out and took Katie's hand. They held hands for a long moment, trying to reassure each other.

"Everyone keeps telling you that investing is a long-term strategy and if you stick with it you'll do okay in the long run. But when the market is right back where it was ten years ago, that 'long-term' business doesn't wash."

"Wall Street doesn't want you to know that over the past eighty years it's been the norm, *not* the exception, for the stock market to stall for painfully long periods of time. In fact, if the market *only* ends up going nowhere for ten years this time, that would be short by historical standards," Jack explained, adding, "In 1981, the Dow ended up right back where it was *seventeen years* earlier. And after the market crashed in October 1929, there was a six-month 'sucker' rally, and then the Dow continued tanking, ultimately taking three years to bottom out, down a staggering 89 percent. Want to guess how long it took for the market to return to its pre-crash level?"

"Fifteen years?" Katie ventured.

"I'd say it took twelve years," Paul said.

"Actually, it took *twenty-five* years. Can you imagine working hard all your life to grow a nest egg, and just as you're about to retire, the market crashes, your nest egg shrivels to a small fraction of what it was, and you don't recover your losses for twenty-five years?"

"It's been tough for a lot of people we know. I had no idea about what you're telling us about how the stock market has done over time," Katie said.

"Most people don't. It's Wall Street's dirty little secret," Jack replied.

Katie asked, "Do you think something like what happened after the stock market crash of 1929 could happen again?"

"I don't know. And neither does anyone else, including all the talking heads on TV and in the magazines and newspapers. And *that's* the problem. Most people pin their hopes for financial and retirement security on things they can't, never could, and never will be able to predict or count on," Jack said, and then, looking at Paul, added, "Like you said, the market has gone nowhere for ten years. But the cost of everything keeps going up. Couldn't you have gotten the same results by putting your money under your mattress and skipped all the nail-biting and sleepless nights?"

"It stinks," Paul replied glumly. "It sounds like that whole 'invest for the long term' thing is just a bunch of hype Wall Street's been feeding us."

"The reality is that most Americans have been digging themselves deeper into a financial hole every year, with *no* way of knowing how long it will take them to crawl out," Jack said.

"Wall Street's dirty little secret is that it's the norm, *not* the exception, for the stock market to stall for painfully long periods of time. During the past decade, you could have gotten the same result stuffing your money in your mattress."

Jack pulled a folder off his desk and held it out to the couple. As Paul took it, Jack said, "A research firm for the financial services industry called Dalbar Inc. studies what kind of returns investors *actu-*

ally get in the stock market. Over the last twenty years, the average equity fund investor outpaced inflation by a mere 1.44 percent. Fixed income investors fared far worse, *losing* their purchasing power by an average of 1.49 percent per year. Asset allocation fund investors have done a bit better, beating inflation, but only by 0.41 percent per year." Jack paused to let it sink in, then asked, "So, is that worth all the worry? That doesn't even factor in the heart-stopping losses we've had in 2008. I'll be surprised if *all* the numbers aren't negative when Dalbar releases its next report."

Katie jabbed Paul with her elbow. "I *told* you we shoulda gone to Vegas. We probably wouldn't have come out any worse, and at least we might have had some fun doing it."

"Yeah, no kidding," admitted Paul. "But we just did what we've all been taught is the best way to save for retirement. What I don't understand is why almost no one, including us, is getting anywhere close to the long-term returns of the market."

"I think it's because people buy and sell at the wrong time," Katie ventured.

"Exactly," Jack said. "Too many folks 'chase performance'—they buy what's been doing great over the recent months, so they get in just when the hot run is over, according to the Dalbar Quantitative Analysis of Investor Behavior. An independent advisory rating service, the Hulbert Financial Digest, found that investors tend to be just as bad on the other side of the equation. They'll tell you they never get scared into selling at the wrong time, but the truth is, they do it over and over again."

"That's us," Katie admitted. "We swear up and down we're not going to let our emotions get the best of us, but it's hard not to. We sell after a stock has taken a dive, then we always wait too long to get back in because we've got cold feet."

"Studies show the typical investor is *lucky* to beat inflation over the long term."

"But you're here today because you're tired of gambling with your financial future—am I right?"

"Yes. You get so you hate listening to the news," Paul said. "There's a terrorist attack somewhere, the market takes a tumble. The Fed adjusts the interest rate and the market goes up. They adjust it again and the market goes down. It just seems like there's no logic to it and you can't win. You feel like it's totally out of your control and you can't predict anything. I *really* don't like that feeling."

"Before I discovered B.O.Y.," Jack said, "I did quite a bit of investment management. When the market went up, my clients were happy, and when it was down, they blamed me. Now I *know* there's a much better way, and I feel sorry for people whose whole financial future still depends on a daily roll of the dice. It just doesn't have to be like that. And besides," he added with a smile, "now my clients love me *every* day."

"That's what we want, too. I don't want any more of these wide-awake nightmares that if something happened to Paul, I'd end up being a bag lady."

"Okay—now we've got two new financial goals to add to your list—make sure you have a retirement income you can count on and predict, and make sure Katie is provided for if something should happen to you, Paul," Jack said. "Do I have it right?" They both nodded in agreement.

Jack continued, "Designing a B.O.Y. plan is a little like when it's time for a new suit. You don't call the store and say, 'I need a suit. Please have one ready for me to pick up when I come by around two o'clock.' There are all those issues of size, and color, and style. And when you've picked out the one you want, it still has to be tailored to fit. Bank On Yourself is the same way. No two plans are exactly alike, and my job is to tailor one so that it fits your situation perfectly."

"You know," Katie said, "I'm glad to hear that. We wouldn't have been very comfortable if you had talked at us for an hour and then asked us to sign a form and write a check for some cookie-cutter plan that's one-size-fits-all."

Jack laughed. He turned to Paul and said, "Your lady knows how to lay it on the line."

"Yep," Paul remarked with just a touch of pride. "She used to be an ambulance dispatcher before she went to work at the hospital as a medical technician. She knows how to size up a situation and say what needs to be said."

With a clear big-picture view of the couple's finances and goals, Jack explained, he would be able to offer some suggestions on how they might restructure their finances to free up money for funding a plan that would help them achieve as many of their goals as possible.

"Most people," Jack said, "come in here thinking they're going to be expected to dig into their pockets for extra money every month. That's uncomfortable, because their budget is already strained. I understand, and a lot of times I can help with that. No promises, but what I always look at first is to see if there's a way you can fund your plan without having to stretch your cash flow farther to do it."

Katie and Paul exchanged a look that seemed to say, "Glad to hear it."

"No two B.O.Y. plans are alike. Each one is custom tailored to the client's unique situation, goals, and dreams. I always look first at ways you could fund your plan without having to stretch your cash flow farther to do it."

With that, Jack began his questions about their financial situation. After about twenty minutes of going over the financial information he had asked them to bring in, he explained the aspects of their finances he would look at to arrive at suggestions for how they could find the seed money to start their B.O.Y. plan. The possibilities, he told them, included reorganizing or restructuring debt, reducing taxes, reducing the funding of 401(k)s and other retirement plans, looking at monthly expenses they might be overpaying for, and making changes to insurance coverage they already have, as well as possible lifestyle changes for them to consider.

When Paul and Katie left twenty minutes later, they agreed on two things: the meeting with Jack had left them both feeling hopeful, and that they were still skeptical that Bank On Yourself could really do for them all the things Jack had suggested it would. However, they were both eager to find out the details of the plan Jack was going to design for them when they came back the following week for their next appointment.

CHAPTER 4

A Flight Plan for Life

*If we did all the things we are capable of doing, we
would literally astound ourselves.*
—THOMAS EDISON

When Paul and Katie returned to Jack's office the following week,
Paul started right off with a jaunty, "So, did you see the stock market
went up 141 points today? That's good news!"

"That's *today's* news," Jack answered. "Are you going to sell your
stocks to lock in your gains?"

Katie gave Paul a long look and then said to Jack, "Did you know
Paul's a terrific market timer? He always knows exactly when the market has topped out and it's time to sell, and exactly when it's hit bottom and we should be buying in again."

Paul laughed a little sheepishly at what was obviously a long-
standing friction between them. Momentarily concerned that the
financial session might get off on the wrong foot, Jack decided to
lighten things up a bit and asked, "Have you heard the new definition
of 'bull market'? It's a random market movement causing an investor
to mistake himself for a financial genius."

"That's my husband," Katie said, pointing at Paul as they both
laughed.

Jack smiled and said, "Then let's make sure that we're all on the same
page about the financial goals and dreams that are most important to
you." He turned over a sheet on an easel that now stood in the corner,
revealing a list of items in bright green felt-tip pen. The list read:

Paul and Katie Harper's Goals
   Emergency cash reserve
   Get back cost of Paul's cars
   Guilt-free vacations to food capitals of the world

Katie's church mission to Africa
Certain, predictable retirement income
Financial peace of mind for Katie if something
happens to Paul

"Did I miss anything?" Jack asked. Both agreed the list included everything they'd discussed the previous week.

"The best news," Jack went on, "is that I've put together a Bank On Yourself program that should allow you to accomplish all six of these short-term and long-term goals and dreams you said were important to you. And you can do it with very little out-of-pocket cost to you. Most of the money to fund your plan will come from simply restructuring financial elements that are already under your control."

"Oh," Katie chimed. "That's great news. To be honest, we thought you were going to tell us we had to cough up an extra couple thousand dollars each month to make this plan work, and we were ready to tell you to forget it."

"Before we're finished here, I think you'll be glad you came in today. Thanks for trusting me this far, at least. To start, I want to show you how the Bank On Yourself plan I've put together for you is going to give you some peace of mind by having a cash reserve you can tap into for an emergency."

Jack's assistant came in with a cup of coffee for Paul and a cup of tea for Katie, as Jack continued. "The way I've designed your plan, just one year after you start, you could have over $17,000 that you can get your hands on to use however you want."

Katie unconsciously moved to the edge of her chair. "Okay, you've got our attention. That would make us feel a *lot* more secure," she said.

"And you won't have to fill out any credit applications, you won't have to beg for a loan, and you won't have the stress of getting cash in an emergency by running up your credit cards. It's money to use whenever you want, for whatever you want."

"Just one year after you start your plan, you could have over $17,000 to use however you want. If an emergency comes up, you won't have the stress of getting cash by running up your credit cards."

The couple exchanged a glance, and Jack continued, "The next item on our list is car loans. By the beginning of the fourth year of your plan—about the time Paul's present car loan is paid off—you could pull $30,000 out of the plan to pay cash for Paul's next car. Then you'll begin making your monthly car payments back to your own plan, which is essentially like making the payments to yourself."

Under item two on the chart, he wrote:

Cars paid from plan.

Jack went on, "From then on, all of Paul's cars could be paid for from the plan. Remember how we talked about how your total cost for a $30,000 car, including interest at the current average rate of 7.5 percent over four years, is nearly $35,000?"

Katie jumped in. "How can we forget?"

"So let's say Paul buys a new car that costs $30,000 after figuring in your trade-in value, and he does it every four years until you both retire, which is six cars. Katie, you're great at doing math in your head. I'll bet you already know how much that comes to, don't you?"

Katie immediately answered, "Yup. That's $210,000 we'd be out. So what would happen if we financed Paul's next six cars through a B.O.Y. plan instead?"

"It's pretty amazing when you use the Spend and Grow Wealthy method," said Jack. "After financing six cars for Paul from the plan and paying the loans back to the plan, you might have something more like $741,000 in your plan when you're ready to retire. Imagine what it would be like if instead of *losing* $210,000 in principal and interest payments, you were *up* $741,000."

"If you finance Paul's next six cars through
your B.O.Y. plan, instead of being
$210,000 poorer, you could have
something more like $741,000 in your plan
when you're ready to retire."

"Wow!" Katie said, wide-eyed. "We could probably retire just on the money that now slips through our fingers for Paul's cars! Would it be double that if I financed my cars using a B.O.Y. plan, too?"

Jack looked pleased and answered, "Maybe not quite double, but close. We'll cross that bridge when we come to it. We haven't even talked about how much bigger your nest egg could be when you finance your dream vacations through Bank On Yourself."

Katie's eyes lit up even more. "I can hardly wait to hear about that part."

By now Paul was becoming eager to get started. He asked Jack, "So I'd need to wait about three years to use B.O.Y. to finance my next car? I can live with that—it's when I'll be ready to buy my next one, anyway."

"Bank On Yourself does take a little patience and discipline," Jack said. "Think of it as a start-up phase, while you're building up the value of your plan. It's a lot like starting a business—the You Finance Yourself Company. It doesn't happen overnight. But being patient during the start-up phase pays a *lifetime* of benefits—getting back the cost of your cars and vacations while growing a nest egg you can predict, and all the rest."

"Makes sense," said Paul.

"But there's something else worth knowing about how a B.O.Y. plan works," Jack continued. "Let's say that in a year or two you decide you want to borrow some money from your plan to make a smaller purchase—like for a trip to the beach or a home repair. You could do that and still have enough to buy a car, as long as you pay the loan back by the time you're ready to buy your next car. And if you pay back your loans the 'Spend and Grow Even Wealthier' way I'll show you, you could actually end up having *more* money than if you *didn't* use your plan to finance things."

"This is sounding better by the minute," Katie smiled.

"But I'm just getting around to the really good stuff, Katie. Your third goal was guilt-free trips to the food meccas of the world, and you wanted to start with Paris, right?"

Katie stood up and crossed to the easel. She picked up a felt-tip pen and drew an arrow, moving the church mission to Africa into position number three. Saying, "I want to switch the priorities," she renumbered the two items. To her husband she said, "I keep thinking about how Judy was changed by her time in Africa. I don't think I could enjoy Paris until I've made one of those church trips myself."

As she sat down, Paul announced with a smile, "The lady has spoken."

"Not a problem," Jack said. "Katie, you can use your plan to cover all your travel costs—clothing, airfare, food, lodging, and everything else. Even household expenses to cover your loss of salary while you're away. I don't know exactly what that total comes to, but I'm estimating you could probably be packing your bags in about a year."

Though Katie didn't speak, she reached out and gave her husband's hand a squeeze. Jack went on, "So that brings us back to the gourmet vacations. I had my assistant do some checking online for a one-week vacation to Paris, with airfare, a nice hotel near the Champs-Élysées, transportation, sightseeing, plus meals including dinners at a couple of top-rated restaurants. And even a day of hands-on classes for Katie at the Cordon Bleu Cooking School."

Paul stopped him. "You were figuring this for two people, I hope. Sounds too good to miss."

Jack was amused. "I wasn't sure whether you would insist on doing Africa with her, but I guessed you wouldn't pass up Paris. The pair of you should be able to do this in only three years, if Katie wants to go to Africa next year first."

Katie's eyes lit up. "I didn't expect we'd be able to do anything like that in the next *ten* years. Being able to do it in only three years would be totally amazing!"

"And if there aren't any other big-dollar items you decide to use your plan for instead, it looks as if you could count on a gourmet food vacation about every two years after your trip to Paris, ticking off all the places on your wish list, wherever your hearts—and taste buds—want to go."

"Let's be realistic, though," Paul said. "Number five on the list—'certain, predictable retirement income'—that's got to be the biggie. Except for the emergency fund, these other things all just go out the window if it's an either/or."

Jack smiled. "Oh, I'm in touch with your priorities. They're very similar to the priorities of most of the people I've done plans for—including my own. Remember that a key advantage of B.O.Y. is that it allows you to enjoy life's luxuries today while still growing your nest egg for tomorrow. It's not an either/or."

"It's hard to fully enjoy a vacation when
you know you'll be paying for it for what
seems like forever. When you finance things
through a B.O.Y. plan, the guilt vanishes
because B.O.Y. lets you enjoy life's luxuries
today while still growing your nest egg for
tomorrow. It's not an either/or."

He went on, "Again, I'm not talking about spending beyond your means. Last week you told me that you feel guilty putting your vacations on credit cards. A lot of people feel that way. It's hard to fully enjoy a vacation when you know you'll be paying for it through the nose for what seems like forever."

Katie nodded her agreement.

"But when you take vacations using your B.O.Y. plan, you'll pay cash for them and make your payments to your plan instead of to a credit card company, so you're getting back the full cost of each vacation, along with the interest you would have paid to the credit card company, and then some. If you were paying for trips to Paris, Hong Kong, and Rome that way, would you still feel guilty about it?"

"I can't imagine that I would, if I'm getting the cost of it back," Katie said. "But one thing still bothers me."

"What's that?" Jack asked.

"Where are you going to find room to put up our pictures?" Both the men laughed, and Jack promised, "I'll put up a picture from you even if I have to add another wall. But I have more good news for you: as a result of using your B.O.Y. plan to finance Katie's mission to Africa and your trips to Paris and other gourmet capitals every couple of years, you could have an additional half-million dollars or more in your plan by the time you retire. That's on *top* of the almost $750,000 you could have by running Paul's next six car purchases through your B.O.Y. plan!"

Katie had to make sure she was hearing this right. "You're talking about Paul and me having something like $1,250,000 in our plan when we retire, *because we're financing six of Paul's cars and our vacations through it?* And we don't have to make risky investments in stocks or real estate to do it?"

"You're talking about Paul and me having
something like $1,250,000 in our B.O.Y.
plan when we retire, *because we're financing six
of Paul's cars and our vacations through it?* And
we don't have to make risky investments in
stocks or real estate to do it?"

"That's the magic of B.O.Y.," Jack explained. "Remember that the money you take out for a car or a trip or whatever isn't a lump of money that disappears from your retirement stash. You treat it like a loan. You repay your plan in installments every month, just like you would be required to do if you borrowed the money from a bank or used a credit card."

Jack continued, "One of the big differences between taking the money out of a B.O.Y. plan and taking it out of a savings or retirement plan is that your B.O.Y. plan will keep growing as though you never pulled a dime out of it."

"I remember that part. It's sinking in," Katie said. "So how much income could we take from the plan when we retire?"

"Based on the analysis I did for you, you could be able to start taking around $70,000 a year from your plan from the day the two of you retire—which you said you wanted to do when you both turn sixty-eight—until you're one hundred. And whatever your 401(k)s may be worth would be on top of that."

"Age one hundred?" Katie looked surprised.

"I always figure it to one hundred," Jack explained. "People are living longer, and I'd rather plan based on you living to one hundred than to eighty-five and have your money run out before you do."

"Well, unless my math is off, which I doubt," Katie said with a laugh, "if we take $70,000 a year for thirty-three years from the time we're sixty-eight until we're one hundred, *that's a total of $2,310,000!*"

"You're right on, Katie," Jack assured her. "That's because your plan continues to grow even while you're taking income, of course."

"So what are those numbers based on?" Paul asked.

Jack explained, "This is a really critical piece of the puzzle. A B.O.Y. plan is *guaranteed* to grow by a contractually set amount every year. The guaranteed increases you receive are based on a 'worst-case' financial results scenario projected by the insurance company. Then, at the end of each year, the company does an accounting of the death claims paid, their earnings, and the expenses of running the company, and the premiums it collected. If they did better than their worst-case projection, they pay the policy owners a dividend."

"So how often do these companies pay dividends?" Katie challenged.

"That's the astonishing part," Jack answered. "You're not guaranteed to receive a dividend every year, but the companies I use have paid dividends every single year for over one hundred years, including during the Great Depression and every market correction. They're very good at under-promising and over-delivering."

"That's very reassuring," Paul said at the same time that Katie, with a tinge of excitement in her voice, said, "It doesn't get much better than that."

"I'm sure you've heard or seen the disclaimer 'past performance is no guarantee of future performance,' and that's true of a B.O.Y. policy, too. However, 'every single year for over a hundred years running' is a pretty darn good track record."

"There can't be very many companies that can make a claim like that," Paul said.

"Keep in mind that your plan is guaranteed to increase by at least the minimum set amount each year. The dividend is the icing on the cake. And once your guaranteed minimum increase or a dividend is credited to your plan, it can't be snatched away by changes in the market," Jack explained. "Imagine what it would be like not to have to depend on luck, skill, or picking the right stocks, funds, bonds, and other investments to grow a nest egg you can count on."

A B.O.Y. plan is *guaranteed* to grow by a contractually set amount every year. And if the company's financial results perform better than its worst-case projections, it also pays policy owners a dividend. Once credited to your plan, neither can be snatched away by changes in the market. Can you imagine what it would be like not to have to depend on luck, skill, or guesswork to grow a nest egg you can count on?

Katie turned to Paul. "Imagine the savings in headache and indigestion pills alone." Jack wondered which one of them got the biggest headaches over their investments.

"My clients tell me they don't miss having to think about how and where their money is invested," Jack said, then remembered that Paul was the one picking the stocks, with Katie being the critic of his choices. "So when I said that your B.O.Y. plan would throw off $70,000 a year for your retirement, that's based on the company's current dividend scale."

Jack went on, "Remember that unless the tax laws change, there is a way to take that annual income without owing taxes on it. If you were in the 33 percent tax bracket after you retire, and had to live off income from your 401(k)s, where you pay tax on your withdrawals, they'd have to throw off about $104,000 a year before taxes—that's an extra $34,000 a year—to equal what you could get from your B.O.Y. plan. How confident are you that your 401(k)s can do that?"

"Not very, given that we've been going backward in them and have no way to predict where they'll be in five years, or fifteen years, for that matter," Katie replied.

"Let me ask you another question," Jack continued. "What direction do you think taxes will go long-term?"

"That's a no-brainer," replied Paul. "I'd bet they're gonna go up."

"That's a pretty safe bet, when you consider the aging demographics of our country, along with the fact that both Social Security and Medicare are heading toward bankruptcy," Jack agreed. "So having a plan that might let you take out your money without owing taxes when you retire would be a blessing."

"Definitely," Paul agreed.

Katie was starting to have trouble hiding her growing impatience. "Look, that's all fine," she said. "But you told us we'd be able to pay for all this without crippling our current lifestyle. I want to find out how that's possible."

"Yeah," Paul added. "It reminds me of an old Steve Martin joke: how do you become a millionaire? First, get a million dollars. . . . Is *that* what you're gonna tell us?" Their laughter broke the tension, but Jack could see Paul was as concerned as Katie.

"I think you're going to be very pleasantly surprised," Jack answered. "The way I've structured your plan, you'll actually be starting with two separate B.O.Y. policies, one for each of you. When we were reviewing your finances, you both mentioned that you'd consider limiting your 401(k) contributions to what your employers match, and putting the difference into B.O.Y. plans. Did I hear that right?"

Katie answered first. "We're just tired of seeing the money we work so hard for disappear the way it's been doing in our 401(k)s."

Paul added, "If B.O.Y. can really do everything you and Rob say, and we can enjoy a better lifestyle when we retire, that's where we'd like our money to start going as soon as possible."

"Okay. I've also looked over the credit card bills you left with me," Jack said. "By restructuring your credit card debt, I've found that you could save a very tidy sum that could also go into your plan every month."

"How much is 'a very tidy sum'?" Katie asked.

Jack said, "Three hundred eighty dollars a month."

Paul whistled.

"I thought you'd like that," Jack said. "Okay, so those are the two places where the lion's share of the money to fund your plans is going to come from. That's money that won't have to come out of your monthly living expenses. Now, you said at our first meeting that you thought you might be able to pull some funds out of your current cash flow, to be used toward a vacation fund."

"We've been talking about that," Paul answered. "There's a little belt-tightening we can do." He looked at Katie, who picked up the ball. "We took a hard look at some of our monthly expenses including our cable bill and found we've been paying for a whole bunch of stations we never watch. That's $40 a month right there. The other item I had to twist Paul's arm about: he's been giving me a birthday present every year of an expensive ring or bracelet or pin. I made him admit that he's been squirreling away $170 a month to save up for it."

"Katie said she'd rather see that money going toward our vacations instead of jewelry," Paul said. "I've enjoyed giving her that jewelry and seeing her wear it. But, yes, I get it about the vacations being more important to her."

"All of these dollars you're freeing up are going to work much harder for you in your B.O.Y. plans than if you parked them in a savings or money market account, or a CD, or a 401(k) or IRA. When you add up all these changes, you'll have $1,000 a month to put into

Paul's plan, and $750 a month for Katie's. I've pulled all the details together about the sources of funds for you to review," he said, picking up a couple sheets of paper from his desk and handing one to each.

"The one financial goal you mentioned last week that I haven't addressed yet is Katie's concern that she'll be financially secure if, God forbid, something should happen to you," Jack said, looking at Paul.

"One of the benefits of a B.O.Y. plan is that if you die before you've finished funding the plan, the company pays a lump sum. So your loved ones can end up getting the money you had *planned* to save, too. As soon as your B.O.Y. plans have been finalized, Katie, you would get around $270,000 from Paul's plan if something were to happen to him, and Paul, you could receive around $260,000 if something happened to Katie."

"And that's on top of everything else you told us about?" Katie asked.

"Yes," Jack said, "because, as Rob told you, we do use a specially designed little-known type of 'whole life' insurance policy for this. You won't hear about this kind of policy from most insurance agents, financial advisors, or the media gurus. You're not buying it just for the death benefit, but also for all the advantages you get from it while you're alive. Still, it's amazing how important it is to many people to have the peace of mind the death benefit gives them."

"If you die before you've finished funding your B.O.Y. plan, the company pays a lump sum. So your loved ones can end up getting the money you had *planned* to save, too. You're not buying this plan just for the death benefit, but it's amazing how important the peace of mind it gives you is to many people."

"Frankly," Paul said, "I've been a little uncomfortable about this insurance business ever since Rob mentioned it. A lot of people say that life insurance is a bad investment."

Jack explained, "A B.O.Y. life insurance policy isn't an investment at all, thankfully. If it was, you'd have to worry about whether your money was even going to be there when you needed it. You made it clear to me that you feel you already have enough of your money at risk in investments you can't count on. The special type of insurance policy we use has been one of wealthy Americans' best-kept financial secrets for a long time. But you don't have to be rich to benefit from it."

Both Paul and Katie were listening intently. Jack leaned forward and continued, "I'm going to let you in on one of the secrets of life insurance that almost no one knows. I've reviewed your current life insurance policies. They're good policies for doing exactly what you bought them for: giving you a financial security blanket if one of you should die an untimely death. But a Bank On Yourself life insurance policy is something different.

"Let me ask you both a question: if you were buying a life insurance policy for the reasons most people buy them—the death benefit, in case something happens to you—and you wanted to get $250,000 worth of coverage, for example, you'd want to pay the lowest premium possible for it, right?"

Paul spoke up. "Yeah. Why would we pay any more than we had to?"

"That's exactly how almost everybody thinks about life insurance—they want the maximum death benefit for the least amount of money. But I'll bet you didn't know that buying a policy that way causes your equity or 'cash value' in the policy to grow at the *slowest* possible rate." Jack paused to see their reaction.

"We didn't even think about the cash value when we bought our policies," Katie said.

"It's fine to buy life insurance that way *if* you're buying it mainly for the death benefit," Jack explained. "But the whole point of Bank On Yourself is to be able to use the policy as a financial management tool from day one. We want your cash value to grow as quickly as possible, because the faster that happens, the sooner you can begin using the policy to get back the money you spend on your cars, vacations, and other major purchases."

Katie said, "It's a life insurance policy, but you don't have to die to win. Is that it?"

"Exactly!" Jack said. "And what a great way to put it."

"You know," Paul said, "I subscribe to two financial magazines and I've read maybe half a dozen books about personal finance. And I've never come across anything that comes even close to what you're describing."

"There are several reasons you won't read about this in the mainstream media. For one thing, it requires a very specific type of policy, and it has to be structured a very specific way. Out of over 1,500 life insurance companies, only a handful even offer the kind of policy that works best with B.O.Y. In fact, the policy we use is so little-known that it isn't even covered in most insurance-industry training programs."

> "B.O.Y. requires a very specific type of
> policy structured a very specific way. Out of
> over 1,500 life insurance companies, only a
> handful offer the right kind of policy. It's so
> little-known that it's not covered in
> insurance-industry training programs,
> which is part of the reason you haven't
> heard of it. With this kind of policy, you
> don't have to die to win."

"So how did you find out about it?" Paul asked.

"I managed to be in the insurance and financial services business for almost twenty years before I stumbled onto Bank On Yourself. I've talked to a lot of other financial advisors since then, and I'd guess that *maybe* one out of a thousand really understands how it works. Most advisors have never even heard of it. And some who have look at it and think the effort of explaining the benefits to folks like you doesn't generate enough commission to be worthwhile spending time on. Helping a client start a B.O.Y. policy means taking an average of a 50 percent cut in commissions you'd make if you sold them the kind of policies most advisors sell."

"So how can you afford to do it?" Paul challenged.

Jack pointed at the photo of Mike and Christina in Paris that he had shown them on their last visit. "Guess how many B.O.Y. policies that couple in front of the Eiffel Tower have started so far."

"Two?" Katie offered.

"Actually, they have six policies now. One for what they call their dream-vacation fund. Two others they're using to get back the cost of both of their cars and to make sure they have a rock-solid retirement plan. They started a fourth and fifth policy a few years back to pay for college for their two kids. And the sixth one they started just last year so they can use it to finance equipment for Mike's medical practice. He used to lease the equipment but got fed up with seeing all that money fly out the window."

Jack went on to explain that the couple had already started working with him on setting up a seventh plan. "The ultimate goal of B.O.Y.," he said, "is to use it to get back the cost of your entire lifestyle. Why stop at just getting back the cost of cars and vacations? That's why couples like Mike and Christina use so many plans."

Jack added, "Like many of my clients, Mike and Christina have already referred a number of friends, coworkers, and relatives to me, without me even asking. That never happened to me before I started helping my clients implement Bank On Yourself. I think most people would rather have a root canal without anesthesia than meet with a life insurance agent."

Katie laughed. Even Paul flashed a grin before tossing another challenge. "I still don't really get what's so special about this type of policy."

"The kind of policy we use for B.O.Y.," Jack began, "is a whole life insurance contract with some special features. For one thing, it has to be a dividend-paying policy. And then we add what's called a paid-up additions rider, or PUAR, to the policy. This *significantly* accelerates the growth of the cash value in your plan, which is great for you, of course."

Jack paused for a moment as if uncertain. "I can explain how adding the PUAR makes that happen, if you want. It's actually a pretty simple explanation."

Paul looked at Katie, passing the decision to her. "Sure," she said. "We want to understand what gives B.O.Y. the power you claim it has."

Jack noticed that Paul had taken out a piece of paper and was ready to take notes.

"The premium you pay each year into the kind of policy we use for B.O.Y. is basically divided into two parts. A portion of that premium goes into traditional life insurance, which is also referred to as the base policy. Instead of making one larger payment upfront for the base policy, you make a series of smaller payments over time—kind of like an installment plan.

"The other portion of your premium in a B.O.Y. plan goes into the paid-up additions rider—which also buys a death benefit, but with several differences. For one thing, what you pay into the PUAR in any year is all the premium you'll ever pay for the death benefit it purchased, which is why it's called 'paid-up.' Then, the next year, what you put into the PUAR buys you more life insurance you'll never pay another premium for. And the same thing happens every time you make a premium payment into the PUAR."

"Okay, I'm following you so far. But how does the PUAR make your cash value grow faster?" Katie asked.

Jack explained, "The simple answer is that the PUAR buys a small amount of insurance, and even if the insured died soon after the premium was paid, the company has already collected enough premium to cover much of the cost of the death benefit the PUAR purchased. That means that now the company has very little risk for that portion of the death benefit, unlike with the base portion of the policy, where they might have to pay out $250,000, even if they've only collected, say, $1,000 in premiums for it. Any idea what that might mean for the policyholder?"

This time it was Paul who saw where this was going. "If the company has covered most of its risk on the death benefit, they can afford to let your cash value grow faster?" he asked.

Jack looked pleased. "Exactly," he said. "I like to call a B.O.Y. policy 'turbo-charged,' and this is where that turbo power comes from. The PUAR grows your cash value in the most efficient way possible. Does that answer your question, Katie?"

"Adding the paid-up additions rider, or PUAR, is like putting your policy on legal steroids—it grows your cash value in the most efficient way possible."

"It does," Katie replied. "But if the PUAR is such a great thing, why can't we just load up the plan with more of the PUAR and less of the base premium, or just have *all* the premium go to the PUAR?"

"That's a very good question, Katie. The IRS determines how much PUAR premium can go into any given policy. If you overstep that limit, the policy becomes what's known as a modified endowment contract, or MEC, and loses the tax benefits a life insurance policy has."

Paul asked, "So, what are the tax advantages of a B.O.Y. policy?"

"You know the old joke about the guy who hears a knock on his door, opens it, and there's a man who says, 'I'm from the IRS and I'm here to help you'?" Jack responded.

"Yeah, right!" Katie laughed, at the same time Paul said, "Not hardly."

"Well, I happen to believe the IRS *is* trying to help you. And here's one of the ways they do it," Jack explained. "Now, keep in mind I'm not a CPA or an accountant, and I like to keep things simple. But here's the lowdown. Remember we talked about how you receive dividends when the company's financial results are better than its worst-case projections?"

Both nodded. "Well," Jack continued, "under current law, dividends you leave in your policy are not taxable. And get this: you can leave those dividends in the plan so that they buy more fully paid-up life insurance, which, like we were just talking about, is life insurance you'll never have to pay another premium for. And that makes your cash value grow at an even *faster* clip. Meanwhile, if you do take some or all of the dividends out of your policy, like when you're ready to take retirement income, they aren't taxed until they exceed your cost basis."

"The amount we've paid into the policy," Katie said.

Jack was impressed. These two were sharp as tacks.

"Yes. And even then," Jack went on, "there's a way to take out more money without paying taxes on it. You just simply switch to borrowing your cash value, because there are no taxes due on policy loans. What this means is that it's possible to get your hands on the equity in your policy without owing taxes, if you do it right."

"Under current tax law, dividends you leave in your policy are not taxable. Dividends you withdraw aren't taxed until they exceed your cost basis, at which point you can switch to borrowing your cash value with no taxes due on policy loans. This is how you can get your hands on your equity in a B.O.Y. plan without owing taxes."

"You see," continued Jack, "a B.O.Y. plan is taxed more like a Roth-type plan, where you pay taxes before you make your contribution, and then you can pull out your money tax-free. I'd just as soon pay the taxes upfront, anyway—I know what my tax rate is now. If I wait till I retire, I might pay higher taxes on a bigger number."

"Okay, we get it," Katie said. "But that doesn't mean we'll know exactly what to do when the time comes."

"That's *my* job, as your Bank On Yourself coach. I usually meet with all my clients twice a year. That way I can help you make wise decisions about when and how to use the money in your plans, how to pay your plan back to maximize the growth of your cash value, when to take loans and when to take dividend withdrawals, and ultimately, the best and most tax-efficient way to take retirement income from your plans."

"Suppose they change the tax laws?" Katie asked.

"Yeah," Paul added. "They change the tax laws every year, don't they?"

"They could change the tax laws, of course. For that matter, they could change the tax laws for retirement plans, including Roth plans. But the tax benefits of a B.O.Y. plan are an *extra*. Even if they disappeared completely, the B.O.Y. method stands on its own and you'd *still* get all the other benefits we've been talking about. From—"

"Wait, wait," Paul interrupted. "Let me see." He started putting up a finger for each one. "We get back the cost of major purchases, we can borrow on the equity in the plan to buy cars or take trips or whatever . . ."

Katie chimed in, "Plus the money we take out keeps on growing as if it was still in the plan . . ."

"And we pay back the policy loans to ourselves, so it's not money out the window," Paul said. "We'll be using all those dollars we're getting back to have a retirement income we can count on."

Katie added, "And we won't go backward when the market tanks *and* we have that death benefit to fall back on, in case something happens to either one of us."

"What do the teachers call that—a pop quiz? Except it was self-imposed. And you each get an A." Jack laughed. "The point is that the tax benefits are like the cherry on top of the banana split."

"The tax advantages of B.O.Y. are an
extra. Even if the tax laws change, B.O.Y.
stands on its own and you'd *still* get
all the other benefits."

Paul saw an opening for a question he'd been wanting to ask. "This business about how the money you've borrowed keeps earning—you said last time you'd explain how that works, and we've both been wondering about that."

"This is a great time to cover that," Jack said. "When you borrow against your cash value, the money doesn't actually come out of your policy. It comes out of the company's general fund. Life insurance is kind of a group effort—all the money in the policies is being pooled together. It may help to use the analogy of a certificate of deposit, or CD, or savings account. If you had your money in a savings account at a bank, they make money by lending it back out to someone else. But of course they would continue paying you the same interest they promised they would, right?"

Paul glanced at Katie, then said, "We're following you so far."

"The difference is that when you borrow against your cash value in your policy, *you're* the place where the money is being loaned. It makes little difference to the insurance company where they put the money to work. Loans they make to *any* source will ultimately increase the cash value of all policies, including yours."

Katie looked puzzled. "Yes . . . but if we have money in a savings account at the bank, and we take it out to buy a car or whatever, it's not earning any interest for us anymore. I still don't get how this is different." She glanced at her husband, who gave a small shrug, meaning, "Neither do I."

"That's what I'm trying to explain. The companies we use for B.O.Y. don't differentiate between whether *you're* using your money in the plan or someone *else* is. Either way, your cash value will continue to grow by the same preset and guaranteed amount every year, and you'll receive the exact same dividends in every year that the company's financial results exceed its worst-case projections, even if you've taken a policy loan," Jack explained.

"Which they have for a hundred years," Paul said.

Jack nodded.

Katie was listening intently. "Oh, I get it now. So *that's* how our money can do double duty for us—growing at the same pace even when we've taken some out to go on a trip to Paris."

Jack said, "That's it. This has got to be the *ultimate* money leverage—probably even more powerful than compound interest. But don't go calling all your friends and saying, 'Hey, you can borrow money from your life insurance and still be earning the same dividends on it.' Because there's one more thing I should mention.

"Most life insurance companies are what's known as direct-recognition companies. They *do* care whether you've taken a loan, and they'll credit your policy a different dividend if you have any loans outstanding. But the companies we like to use for B.O.Y. are *non*–direct recognition companies, and they credit you the exact same dividend regardless of whether you've taken a policy loan. They simply 'don't recognize' that you've borrowed from your plan when they pay dividends. And if you die with any loans unpaid, the company will simply deduct the loan balance and any interest due on the loan from the death benefit, which is used as collateral for any loans you take."

"Certain life insurance companies known as non–direct recognition companies credit you the exact same dividend regardless of whether you've taken a policy loan—so your money can work much harder for you."

"So the company we have our current life insurance with probably wouldn't treat a policy loan the same way—is that what you're saying?" Paul asked.

"Not many companies do, Paul," Jack replied. "There just aren't many companies that make the grade for the purposes of Bank On Yourself. It has to be a company that issues policies that are dividend-paying whole life insurance and that incorporate a *flexible* paid-up additions rider to maximize the growth of your cash value. On top of that, it has to be a non–direct recognition company, as I just mentioned, and it has to have a great long-term track record of paying dividends. And, of course, it should be one of the top life insurance companies in terms of financial strength, as determined by the independent ratings services, so you know your money will be safe.

"We insist on *all* of these requirements for you so that your cash value will grow fast, which allows you to use it sooner. You'll have maximum flexibility, you'll get the same dividends even if you've taken loans from your plan, and you'll gain all the available tax advantages."

To give you all the advantages and benefits described here, a B.O.Y. policy should be from a life insurance company that meets *all* these requirements:

· Dividend-paying whole life
· Offers a flexible PUAR
· Non–direct recognition, so your policy grows at the same rate when you borrow against your cash value
· Great long-term track record of paying dividends
· Very strong financially, as determined by independent rating services

---

The melody of the Beatles' "Hey, Jude" broke the mood. "Sorry," Paul mumbled as he took out his cell phone and flipped it open to see who was calling. "Sorry," he said again, louder, "but I need to take this," and he walked out of the room.

When he came back several minutes later, Katie noticed he looked troubled. He leaned over and spoke softly to her. "We just lost our biggest account, and I have to cut back on staff. I've got to lay somebody off." To Jack he said, "I don't like running out on you in the middle, but it can't be helped. I'll call about rescheduling to continue —hopefully next week, if we can make all three calendars fit."

He was already starting out the door, Katie at his heels, looking concerned.

Jack didn't know what to think. He had been pleased with their quick understanding of Bank On Yourself. And now, suddenly, they were gone. He wondered if he'd really see them again the following week.

CHAPTER 5

The New World of Money

*The dumbest people I know
are those who know it all.*
—Malcolm Forbes

Jack Richards was pleased when Katie called a few days later to reschedule. When the couple walked back into his office the following week, Jack discovered that the reason for the sudden walk-out was the topic at the top of Paul's agenda.

"I've never had to lay anybody off before," Paul said as the couple took their seats. "You hear on the news that some giant company is downsizing and laying off two thousand people, and you think, 'Those poor guys, turned out on the sidewalk.' And then the pinch hits your own company, and you find *you're* the S.O.B. who's gotta pick somebody to let go and tell the bad news to."

He paused to take a drink of water. Jack saw that Paul really needed to get this off his chest. "The most junior guy on my team had been with us for six years. Chuck Langston. *Six years.* It was just like all those sports movies where the coach has to tell a player they're letting him go, and the coach always says it's the toughest thing he's ever had to do."

Paul shook his head, saddened just thinking about it. He went on, "The worst part was when the human resources lady came to talk to me about Chuck's loan against his 401(k). Do you know how a 401(k) loan works? If you leave the company for *any* reason, you have to pay any loans back, in full, with interest, within *sixty days!*"

Jack explained, "It's almost always a very short fuse, and in most cases, thirty to sixty days is all you get. Retirement plans like 401(k)s, IRAs, and defined-benefit plans come with all kinds of restrictions. You can have the loan treated as a distribution, but then you have to pay income taxes on it, and, unless you've reached age fifty-nine and a half, you'll *also* get hit with a 10 percent penalty. That could mean having to pay the IRS as much as 40 percent—or even more—of the amount of the loan you took from your plan."

"Chuck took a $10,000 loan to pay some medical bills for his wife's mother. His wife is having panic attacks about how they're going to manage till Chuck lands another job. He came in to see me when he found out about having to repay that loan. He said, 'I thought the money in my 401(k) was mine and I could use it when I needed to.' He was stunned. I thought he was going to break out in tears. I really felt bad for him, but I was also thinking, 'I'm glad that's not me.'"

"It's been doom and gloom around our house since we last saw you," Katie told Jack. "Paul's always been the kind of manager who went to bat for his people."

"I've seen it happen too many times. Most people just don't realize how all the restrictions and rules plans like 401(k)s have can affect them until it's too late," Jack said. "I can't help but think how much better off Chuck would have been if he'd had his money in a Bank On Yourself plan instead."

Katie said to Jack, "We've been wondering—if he had that loan against a B.O.Y. plan, he wouldn't have had to pay it back?"

"I always encourage my clients to pay their loans back whenever possible. Especially in the very early years of the plan, you do need to be careful about borrowing all your cash value and not paying it back at all. But a B.O.Y. plan gives you a lot of flexibility if something comes up. As I keep saying, it's your money and you can use it how and when you want. So you can pay less on your loan repayments, or skip them altogether for a while. The company won't come after you for the loan, so you wouldn't run into the problem Chuck is having.

"Most people don't realize how all the restrictions and rules plans like 401(k)s have can affect them until it's too late. A B.O.Y. plan gives you lots of flexibility. It's your money and you can use it how and when you want."

"All the company asks is that you pay any interest due on your loans at the end of the policy year. If you don't, they'll simply deduct the interest from your equity in the policy. But that's only *one* of the advantages of a B.O.Y. plan over a 401(k)."

"What else?" Katie asked.

"The percentage of Americans taking loans from their 401(k)s has been spiking, and several recent studies have shown that taking even modest loans can *dramatically* erode your savings over time. One study by Vanguard calculated that a thirty-five-year-old with a $20,000 plan balance who takes out two loans in fifteen years ends up with about $38,000 less at age sixty-five than someone who never borrows, even if the loans are repaid without penalty," Jack explained.

"That's a pretty significant difference," Paul said, adding, "But when you borrow from a B.O.Y. plan and pay the loans back, that doesn't happen, because the money you borrowed continues to grow just the same, right?"

"Exactly. That's one reason we call it the Spend and Grow Wealthy way to buy things. But there are other downsides to 401(k) and other government-sponsored retirement plans that you don't have with B.O.Y. For one thing, there are strict and pretty low limits on how much you can contribute each year to a 401(k), IRA, or the like. You may be able to sock away a much larger amount in a B.O.Y. plan."

This time it was Katie who started jotting down notes.

"Many retirement plans also severely limit the amount you can borrow, and what you can borrow for," Jack went on. "And in most circumstances, you're required to pay the money back within five years, or it becomes taxable and you have to pay the same penalty your employee Chuck is faced with."

Katie said, "Ouch!" Paul added, "I second that."

Jack continued, "With traditional retirement plans, you just don't have the flexibility of a B.O.Y. plan. They've got more strings attached to them than a puppet. If you want to take distributions before you're a certain age, you have to pay penalties, and you're *required* to start taking distributions by the time you're seventy and a half, whether you want or need to. You don't have those restrictions with a B.O.Y. plan. And that's something my clients tell me they really appreciate."

"It'd be nice to be in control of our money, instead of the government pulling all the strings," Katie said.

Jack then asked, "If you wanted to borrow from your 401(k) right now, or if you *had* to, would you have to sell some of your investments to do it?"

"Yes," Katie answered, "but they've been taking such a beating lately, I'm not sure I'd mind selling some."

"But if you did that," Jack answered, "you'd be breaking Rule #1 of investing. You're *supposed* to be buying low and selling high, not the other way around."

Paul said, "But with one of your plans, we wouldn't have to sell any funds, investments, or assets if we needed to borrow, right?"

"Right," Jack agreed, then added, "There's one more advantage we touched on last week. Katie, you said knowing you'd have financial security if something happened to Paul was important to you."

"Of course," she said.

"Remember that as soon as your policies are issued, you'd receive around $270,000, and, Paul, you'd receive around $260,000 if something happened to Katie. The death benefit either of you would receive can be *many* times greater than the current equity in either of your plans. It wouldn't matter if there were only $1,000 of cash value in the policy—the beneficiary would receive the full amount of the death benefit."

Jack continued, "But with your 401(k) plans, all the surviving spouse would get is the current value of the plan. And right now for both of you, that's only a fraction of what you'd receive from the B.O.Y. plans I've designed for you."

"I'd like to think we'll be sitting on the porch in side-by-side rocking chairs well into our nineties," Katie said, "but that's comforting to know."

"One more thing worth knowing about that," Jack continued, "is that the death benefit goes to the beneficiary income tax–free, under current tax law."

"That's good to know, Jack," Paul said.

"Probably the biggest drawback to 401(k)s and IRAs is that they're not guaranteed or assured, and all the risk of making wise investment choices and planning for retirement falls entirely on workers who have no training to deal with it," Jack explained. "It's insane to expect the average person to become a financial analyst or investment genius when studies show that *most* financial experts and mutual fund managers underperform the market—and many do so by a significant margin. Many experts are now acknowledging that 401(k)s are an experiment that has failed miserably."

"I can think of a lot better ways to spend my time than trying to figure out what the market's going to do or how to try to bump up my investment returns a point or two," Paul said and added ruefully, "If most *experts* can't even do it successfully, how am I supposed to be able to do it?"

"That's something you won't have to worry about with B.O.Y.," Jack responded. "Can you imagine what it would be like to know your nest egg is growing predictably, the growth is guaranteed, your principal and gains are locked in, and your plan grows more efficiently every year simply because you stuck with it—with no luck, skill, or guesswork required to make that happen?"

"It would be a huge relief," Paul began. "But there's something that's been bugging me. I don't mean to sound negative, but I was listening to one of my favorite radio stations in the car a few days ago and Dave Ramsey's financial talk show came on. One of the questions a listener asked was about whole life insurance and Ramsey started totally trashing it. For one thing, he said you'd come out ahead putting money in a savings or investment account, and then pay cash for things."

Jack replied, "You can use any number of savings vehicles to put aside funds so you can pay cash for things and then make payments back to that account. For that matter, you could save your money in a tin can or under your mattress, and, in the *short* term, you'd have more money available to you."

Both the Harpers looked surprised.

Jack went on to explain, "In the first couple years, saving that way will beat out saving in a B.O.Y. plan, because you're paying more initial costs of the insurance in the early years of the plan. But you get very handsomely rewarded for your patience, because B.O.Y. plans get better every year you have them. The growth is both guaranteed *and* exponential."

"In the first couple years, saving money in a tin can will beat out saving in a B.O.Y. plan, because you're paying more initial costs of the insurance in the early years of the plan. But you get very handsomely rewarded for your patience, because B.O.Y. plans get better every year you have them. The growth is both guaranteed *and* exponential."

"I'm getting it that the usual savings and investing programs people use don't have the features B.O.Y. does. But another thing Ramsey said about whole life was that you should buy term insurance instead and have the policy cover you until you've saved enough that you don't need it anymore," Paul pressed on. He hoped he wouldn't make Jack feel like he was attacking him personally, but he was determined to get answers to the questions that had come up since he and Katie had met with Jack the previous week.

Katie chimed in then, too. "Suze Orman says the same thing on TV. She says that you should buy term insurance because it's cheaper and if you invest the difference in the stock market, you'll come out ahead."

Jack leaned back in his chair. "I *love* when my clients ask me about this, because it's so easy to prove the 'experts' wrong, it's like falling off a log. You be the judge."

Even Paul, who had arrived in what seemed to be such a down mood, couldn't help smiling at Jack's fervor.

"Most of these gurus, including Suze and Dave, say you shouldn't buy whole life insurance because 'it's more expensive than term life insurance.' But Suze admits in her books that the reason term policies are so much 'cheaper' than whole life policies is that the companies know there's very little chance you'll ever receive any benefit from them. In fact, a study done by a professor of insurance at Penn State University showed that fewer than 1 percent of term policies ever pay a claim. Is there anything more expensive than paying for something you most likely won't get any benefit from?"

"Less than 1 percent?!" Paul said. "That's incredible."

"Look at it this way," Jack continued. "No financial expert I've ever read or heard tells people to rent their home if they can afford to buy one, because every penny you pay for rent is money out the window. Yet buying a term policy is just like 'renting' insurance, and 99 percent of the time you'll have *zip* to show for it."

Buying a term life insurance policy is like renting insurance, and 99 percent of the time you'll have *zip* to show for it. It's designed to terminate before you do.

He went on, "When you buy whole life instead of term, you build equity, you can use your money in the plan and *still* have it working for you, and you can get back every penny of premium you pay in, tax free, as long as the current tax laws remain on the books. If you're interested in recapturing your dollars, you buy a house, you don't rent one. So doesn't it make more sense to own your policy, as you do with whole life, and not just rent it, as you do with term?"

"Makes sense," Paul agreed.

"And that's only *part* of the problem with term insurance," Jack insisted. "The types of term policies these experts typically recommend don't even come with any protection against inflation. That could result in financial suicide for you. Let's say you buy a twenty-year term policy at age forty, with a $250,000 death benefit. If inflation averaged only 4 percent a year in that time, how much of that $250,000 do you think you'd lose?"

Paul ventured a guess. "Maybe 30 percent?"

"Actually, that term policy would lose 56 percent of its value. More than *half!* So you might not end up getting anything close to the financial security you signed on for. And what happens if you outlive the twenty-year term of the policy, as the insurance company knows you most likely will?"

"Then every penny you paid is down the drain," Katie answered. "But that's the point of insurance, isn't it? You spend money for protection that you hope you'll never need. And in those twenty years, I would have had the comfort of knowing that money would be there for Paul if anything happened to me."

"Katie," Jack persisted, "wouldn't you rather have been paying those premium dollars into something that wouldn't leave you empty-handed at the end of twenty years? A policy like the kind I've been talking about, with all the benefits we've been looking at?"

"Well, of course, when it's a choice of one or the other."

Jack had pulled two books off a shelf in the corner of the room and put them on his desk. Paul and Katie both glanced at them and noticed one was by Dave Ramsey, called *The Financial Peace Planner,* and the other was *The Road to Wealth,* by Suze Orman.

Opening to a page in Dave's book, Jack pointed to where Ramsey states that a "level or fixed-rate term policy is the only way to go" and suggests using policies with terms of ten or twenty years. Jack looked at Paul and asked, "If you do that, what would happen if you develop a health problem before the term ends, but it turns out you still need insurance, because you haven't saved enough money yet?"

"I guess I'd have to pay a lot more for a new policy," Paul said.

Jack said, "That's the best-case scenario. The worst case is that you might no longer qualify for coverage at *any* price. To counter against that possibility, though, Suze's solution is to get a term policy that guarantees you'll be able to continue renewing it, even if your health has slipped. What she doesn't mention is that the premiums for those kind of policies get so high that most people in that situation are forced to drop the policy, just when they need protection the most."

Katie laughed. "It sounds like they call it 'term' insurance because it's really designed to terminate before you do!"

Both men smiled, and Jack said, "Well put, Katie. In fact, even the financial gurus like Dave and Suze admit that."

Paul then asked, "Jack, if a whole life policy is so much better than term, how come these five-star experts say it's so bad?"

Jack picked up the Suze Orman book and flipped it open to a page he'd marked. "Referring to whole life insurance, Suze writes, 'Your death benefit is constant . . . for as long as the policy is in effect.'"

Turning to the couple, he said, "Hold that thought, because I'm going to *prove* to you that the experts aren't even talking about the type of policy we use for Bank On Yourself plans." He brought some documents from his desk, sat down near Paul and Katie, and showed them first the original life insurance policy he'd received when he started his first B.O.Y. plan. And then, for comparison, the most recent annual statement for that plan, pointing out that the policy numbers were the same on both documents.

> "I'm going to *prove* to you that the experts aren't even talking about the type of policy we use for Bank On Yourself plans."

Paul was amused, and Katie surprised, that Jack might think they would suspect him of deception, yet each of them checked the policy numbers and satisfied themselves.

"Look at the death benefit when I started the plan," Jack said.

Katie read the figure. "It says $250,000."

"That's what's called the initial 'face amount'—the amount of life insurance or death benefit at the time you *start* the policy. Now take a look at my most recent annual statement. What does it say the current death benefit is now?"

Paul read it aloud. "Current death benefit, $380,863."

"In nine years, the death benefit has increased more than 52 percent. Some of my other B.O.Y. policies have gone up by even more, because they were designed to do that. Almost all the media financial gurus are only talking about policies that *don't* pay dividends. In those policies, the death benefit usually stays level the whole time. They never even discuss the most commonly known type of dividend-paying whole life, which is a completely different animal, let alone the almost unheard-of variation we use for a B.O.Y. policy . . ."

Paul finished the sentence: ". . . that includes a paid-up additions rider." Katie looked at her husband and finished *his* sentence: ". . . which is what 'turbo charges' the policy." Paul flashed an amused look at Katie. "We sound like a comedy team."

Katie smiled back at Paul, then said to Jack, "You know what they say about couples who finish each other's sentences?"

"Uh-oh," Jack said. "And what's that?"

"They've been married too long," Paul answered for Katie.

"See! There you go doing it again," Katie shot back, and they both laughed.

Jack smiled, paused a moment, and then picked up the thread. "Policies with a PUAR are apparently completely unknown to the people who criticize using insurance as a wealth-building tool. And I don't think most of them know about dividend-paying whole life either. Which actually isn't surprising—when I got into the financial services business, I went through a full training program that never even mentioned those types of policies."

> "Policies with a paid-up additions rider (PUAR) are completely unknown to the people who criticize using insurance as a wealth-building tool. And I don't think most of them know about dividend-paying whole life either. Most training programs never even mention those types of policies."

"Well, obviously your death benefit went up dramatically, so it makes sense that they're *not* talking about the same type of policy," Paul noted.

"There's one other possibility to be aware of," Jack continued. "A dividend-paying whole life policy gives you the option of receiving your dividends in cash, instead of leaving them in your policy. If you choose that option, your death benefit *would* stay level, even though it's a dividend-paying policy. It's common to take your dividends in cash when you're taking retirement income from the policy, but it's not very common to do that in the early years of the policy. And any advisor who would recommend that doesn't understand the growth acceleration magic that happens when you leave your dividends in the policy."

"I remember you talked last week about how that works. And that helps clear part of it up," Paul said and then paused. "Look, I don't want you to think we're doubting you, but some people we've mentioned this to raised a couple of issues that Katie and I both want to get cleared up."

"Fire away," Jack said. "I think I've probably heard them all, and I sure don't want you to move ahead until every concern you have is laid to rest and you're confident it's right for you."

"With a whole life policy, from what we were told, when the person dies, the insurance company pays you the death benefit, but they confiscate the cash value—all the equity that's in your policy. Is that true?" Paul asked.

"Actually, your Dave Ramsey says that, too," Jack noted, as he flipped the Ramsey book open again, to the section on the drawbacks of whole life policies. He read out loud: "'Whole life insurance pays only the "face" value when you die . . . the company gets the savings or cash value.' He gives an example of someone buying a $70,000 whole life policy and paying on it until they have $8,000 of cash value, then he says, 'If you die, the insurance company will pay your wife or husband $70,000 and they keep the $8,000.'"

"So is that true?" Paul asked.

"Yes and no. It is *if* you buy a policy that doesn't pay dividends. You'd get just the $70,000 death benefit, using Ramsey's example. You wouldn't also get the $8,000 cash value."

"But it's different for a B.O.Y.-type policy?" Paul asked.

"It's different. *Very* different. It's amazing that so many people, and so many experts, hold whole life insurance to a totally different standard than other financial vehicles. If you have $80,000 of equity in your home and you sell it for $250,000, do you expect to end up receiving both amounts, a total of $330,000?"

Paul said, "I think I see where you're going with this."

Katie looked puzzled. "I'm not sure I'm with you yet."

"Let me give you a different example. What if you paid $10 for a stock and sold it for $11. Would you expect to receive $21 when you sold it?"

Katie shook her head, but her "No, of course not" sounded as if she didn't yet see how the logic applied to the insurance example.

"So why would you expect that a whole life policy would give you the sum of the two amounts?" Jack asked.

"Oh, I get it now," said Katie.

"I guess that *would* be like holding whole life to an unrealistic standard," Paul replied.

"But here's the clincher: a B.O.Y. policy can even deliver that advantage!" Picking up the policy he had shown Paul and Katie, Jack pointed to one line. "On this policy of mine, here's the total current cash value: $116,155. And what's the current total death benefit again?"

Paul said with a smile, "Same as it was five minutes ago: $380,863."

Jack continued, "So if something happened to me on my way home from work today, that's the amount my family would get—$380,863."

"Wait a minute," Katie said, looking surprised. "Let me see if I've got this right. Your initial death benefit was $250,000 and your current cash value is over $116,000. That's a total of over $366,000. But if your family would get a check for over $380,000, they'd be getting *more* than your original death benefit, plus your current cash value! An additional—what? $14,000. Is that right?"

Jack looked pleased. "Close enough, and I rest my case. The point I'm making is that people like Ramsey and Orman and other financial advisors aren't even talking about this kind of policy."

> "If something happened to me on my way
> home from work, my family would receive
> a check for an amount equal to my
> original death benefit, *plus* my current
> cash value, *plus* an additional $14,000.
> That's because both the dividends left in
> the policy and the PUAR have been
> buying additional coverage, while
> growing the cash value in the most
> efficient way possible."

"That's clear to me now," Paul said. "But they sure do give you the idea that *any* kind of whole life insurance is something you should stay far away from."

"It's not that Suze, Dave, and 99.9 percent of the rest of the media gurus and rank-and-file financial advisors are trying to deceive anybody. And they're certainly not stupid. It's just that they don't know about the type of policies we use, because they're not covered in any of the traditional or common training programs for financial advisors and insurance agents. I've always kept an eye out for products and concepts that might give my clients an edge, but it *still* took me twenty years to come across this," Jack explained.

"Jack, now you've got me curious. You say your family would get $14,000 *more* than your policy's initial death benefit plus the current cash value, if something happened to you. But how does that part work?" Katie asked.

"Good question, Katie. The amount my family would get includes all the additional coverage my PUAR has purchased over the years, plus the additional life insurance purchased by the dividends I left in the policy."

"Okay, now I understand how that works," Katie said.

"But there's one concern I still have," Paul put in. "A lot of people say they don't like whole life because the cash value grows so slowly."

"That's true of the kind of *non*-dividend-paying policies that Suze, Dave, and others talk about," Jack said. "You might not have any cash value at all in those policies until the third year or so, and even then the cash value will grow painfully slowly. Frankly, I can understand why the experts don't like those plans.

"Then you have the regular dividend-paying type of policy that some advisors know about—what I like to call a 'plain vanilla' dividend-paying plan. It might have a little cash value after a year and a half. From then on, your cash value will grow faster than it would in a non-dividend-paying policy, but nowhere *near* as fast as it will in a Bank On Yourself–type policy, which is a policy that *maybe* one out of a thousand advisors knows anything about."

Paul asked, "Well, the cash value in my plan would have to grow fast enough that I can buy a car with it in a few years, right?"

"Yes," Jack answered. "The point of B.O.Y. is to be able to use the money to finance things sooner rather than later. So, by adding the paid-up additions rider, you could have cash value in the first year, and it will grow much faster than either of the other two types of policies we've been talking about."

"How *much* faster?" Paul wanted to know.

"I'll show you. I save every policy statement I've ever gotten. I *love* comparing them and watching them grow. Here are the annual statements from the end of the first year from two of my policies," Jack said, pulling out two sheets of paper and spreading them out for the couple to see. "The first statement shows the cash value in a regular, 'plain vanilla' dividend-paying whole life policy I started right before I found out about Bank On Yourself. At the end of the first year, you can see, this policy actually did have a little cash value—all of $176."

Pointing to the second sheet, Jack continued, "The next statement shows the cash value at the end of the first year in the first B.O.Y. turbo-charged policy I started less than a year after I bought the 'plain vanilla' policy. The premium for both policies is the same. See the difference?"

"Wow!" said Paul. "The cash value is $7,282."

"That's *huge!*" Katie exclaimed. "The B.O.Y. plan has something like *forty times more cash value* than the 'plain vanilla' dividend-paying plan."

"By adding the paid-up additions rider, you could have as much as *forty times more cash value* at the end of the first year than you would with a traditionally designed policy."

"Katie, you must have a calculator implanted in your brain," Jack said as they all laughed. "Obviously a B.O.Y. policy grows *much* faster in the early years. Eventually a 'plain vanilla' dividend-paying policy won't trail quite so far behind a B.O.Y. policy as it does in the beginning. But because of the slow start a 'plain vanilla' policy gets, it'll *never* catch up, all things being equal. That's why even after I've had these two policies for thirty-five years, the B.O.Y. policy is projected to have 26 percent *more* cash value."

"And that happens because you designed the B.O.Y. policy so your cash value would grow as fast as possible, instead of having a big death benefit, right?" Katie asked.

"Exactly," Jack said. "But get this: when I'm seventy-five, my B.O.Y. policy is projected to have a 20 percent higher death benefit than my 'plain vanilla' policy!"

Katie looked confused. "How's that possible? I mean, if your premium is the same for both policies, shouldn't your death benefit be a lot lower on the B.O.Y. policy?"

Jack replied. "It happens because of the paid-up additions rider we add to B.O.Y. policies. We talked last week about how every year that you pay the PUAR portion of the premium, it buys you more death benefit *and* turbo charges the growth of your cash value. So you end up getting accelerated growth of your cash value *and* the death benefit, too. And that gives you some built-in protection against inflation on both your cash value and death benefit."

"The difference between these two policies really *is* amazing," Katie agreed.

"With a B.O.Y.-designed policy, you get
accelerated growth of your cash value
and the death benefit, which gives you
some built-in protection against
inflation for both."

"Let me show you something you'll have to look forward to." Jack picked up the statement for the first B.O.Y. policy he had shown Katie and Paul, the one he had started nine years earlier. "Take a look at this line, where it shows how much my cash value increased in the last year. It's more than two and a half times the premium I put in. A dozen years from now I can expect it to increase by more than *five times* my premium, if the dividends stay the same as they are now."

"Just the opposite of what our 401(k) plans are doing," Paul said.

Katie added, "And our home went down over 20 percent in the last year or so. Kinda makes you wonder what else the 'experts' don't know. . . ."

"I think a man named Thomas Kuhn may have put his finger on the answer, Katie. In his book *The Structure of Scientific Revolution,* he wrote that experts resist new paradigms for approximately thirty years—a whole generation. And listen to this: he found that the worst offenders were the experts *within* an industry, who would resist anything that differed from their accepted dogma. So I wouldn't expect Suze, Dave, or the other 'experts' to change their tune anytime soon, even after being confronted with the facts. And given how convinced they are that whole life is a bad thing, do you really think they'd take the time to learn how a B.O.Y. plan is different and then admit they made a mistake trashing *all* whole life policies?"

"Thank you, Jack. This has really been eye-opening," Paul said. "If people don't get to see that there are different types of whole life policies, they could easily come to the conclusion that they should avoid them all. I've learned things today that have completely turned my head around."

"I know it's confusing with all the misinformation out there, and the fact that financial advisors just don't get any training on the type of policies we use for Bank On Yourself. And you've only just met me, so I don't want you to take anything I say for granted. Challenge me; raise *every* question you've got."

With a grin, Katie said, "That's exactly what we're doing."

"Yes, you sure are," Jack agreed, then got up and pointed to one of the pictures on his wall, showing a family vacationing at an amusement park. "Does this setting look familiar?" he asked.

"Disneyland!" they both said together.

"It's another example of how tried and true this method is. Walt Disney borrowed $100,000 from his whole life policy to start Walt Disney Inc. when no bank would lend him the money."

"You mean all those Disneylands everywhere might not exist if it hadn't been for his whole life policy?!" Katie asked.

"Probably not," Jack replied. "He didn't have to answer to a bank about what he was planning to do. Right now a lot of people would like to be in that position. Instead they're receiving notices that their home equity line of credit has been reduced or canceled, effective immediately. Some are being told they must pay their loans back much faster than they had planned. And the credit card companies are reducing the limits on how much you can charge and jacking up the interest rate. People are finding out that they really have little control when using other people's money, and even consumers and businesses with good credit records are finding it difficult—if not impossible—to borrow money."

"Right now it seems like the only people who can get credit are those who don't need it," Katie interjected.

"You got it," Jack said. "But with B.O.Y., you have control, because it's *your* money."

"The best of all worlds, it sounds like," Katie said.

"Yes, and that applies to Bank On Yourself in a number of ways," Jack explained. "You know, I think people have gotten used to the idea that they have to make a choice—like spend their money *or* save for retirement. Or the choice of having their money in a safe but slow-growing plan like a savings account, or having it where it can grow, but without any guarantees or predictability, like your 401(k). That's why B.O.Y.'s combination of flexibility, growth, and security is so appealing. It puts you in the driver's seat. It's the ultimate 'have your cake and eat it too' financial tool."

"Bank On Yourself's combination of control, flexibility, growth, and security makes it the ultimate 'have your cake and eat it too' financial tool."

"How safe is our money in a Bank On Yourself plan? With companies like Lehman, Wachovia, and others failing, it makes you wonder," Paul said.

"Life insurance companies are tightly regulated because of the crucial role they play in ensuring the financial security of families," Jack explained. "They are audited regularly by the insurance commissioners of the states they do business in to make sure they maintain sufficient reserves to be able to pay claims and are on solid ground. If a company fails to maintain proper reserves or gets into financial difficulty, the state insurance commissioner's office can step in, take over the company, and run it in the interests of policyholders. Usually, a failed insurer's business is taken over by another company. They are also audited regularly by several different independent ratings services. And there's yet another layer of protection—each state has an insurance guaranty fund that insures the cash value and death benefit of all policies up to certain limits."

Katie, who had been taking notes, asked, "What about what happened to AIG?"

"What you may not realize is that AIG had hundreds of subsidiaries throughout the world, many of which are insurance-related. But, according to the National Association of Insurance Commissioners, their insurance subsidiaries *did not receive a bailout; they are financially solvent . . .* they did not cause the crisis, rather they will play a crucial role in the solution.'"

Katie looked relieved. "I didn't know that, and what you've just explained is very reassuring."

"There are some things you should know about the company I'll put your B.O.Y. plan with that should also help put your mind at ease," continued Jack. "It's one of only a handful of life insurance companies that offer the kind of policy that meets all the requirements for a B.O.Y. plan. It's a top-rated and very conservative company that doesn't invest in the kind of risky financial products that led to the failure of banks and investment firms. They don't sell any of the 'variable' products that have been in the news. Its parent company has been in business for well over a century and is rated as *one of the financially strongest life insurance groups in the world.* And it's a 'mutual' company. Are you familiar with that term?"

Katie and Paul both shook their heads.

"A mutual insurance company is, in essence, owned by its policy owners, *not* stockholders. That lets them focus on the long-term interests of policyholders, instead of the short-term demands of Wall Street."

"Life insurance companies are tightly regulated and policy owners are protected by several safety nets, including your state guaranty fund. The companies used by Bank On Yourself Authorized Advisors are among the financially strongest life insurance companies in the world."

"It all sounds good," Paul said. "But what's the downside? Nothing in life is 100 percent. I just don't want any surprises down the road. . . ."

"Actually, there are three things anyone considering Bank On Yourself should be aware of," Jack replied without hesitating. "We live in an immediate-gratification society and some people are looking for a quick fix or magic bullet—they want something they can put under their pillow before they go to sleep and wake up rich in the morning.

"The media loves to run stories about the kid who dropped out of college with some kind of software or Internet idea, and practically overnight it became the next Google. Well, great, but for most of us, it just ain't gonna happen that way. Not with B.O.Y. and not with anything else. That's the first 'catch,' if you want to call it that."

"Jack," Paul said, "we already know there aren't any magic pills. If we can start taking the overseas vacations every couple of years that Katie's been dreaming of, starting only three years from now, that'll be pretty darn good."

"It's more than 'pretty darn good,'" Katie added. "In my wildest dreams I had never imagined that would be possible on what we make now. And that's on top of being able to go on the mission to Africa in a year." Then, turning to Jack, she pressed on. "But you said there were three things. What else?"

"B.O.Y. is a long-term strategy. If you decide to cancel and cash out your plan in the first couple years, you won't get back every dollar you put in. There's a cost for all the advantages and guarantees that come with a B.O.Y. plan, and you pay more initial costs of the insurance in the early years," Jack explained. "That's the start-up phase we talked about—the one-time requirement that pays a lifetime of benefits. If you have a little patience, you get richly rewarded, since the plan grows more efficiently every year you have it. Dropping out doesn't make any sense."

"So why would someone drop out?" Katie asked.

Jack shrugged. "Who knows? For some, it's probably for the same reason people who start a diet program drop out if they haven't lost ten pounds by the end of the first month. Or their Aunt Etta, who used to write about finance for the *Paducah Times*, tells them it was a bad decision, even though she knows nothing about Bank On Yourself."

"No 'Aunt Ettas' on either side of our family," Katie laughed.

"And we're not going to listen to anybody who doesn't know the facts about Bank On Yourself," Paul added. "No problem with your first two points. What's number three?"

"Number three is, I need to warn you there are going to be times when you feel left out." They both looked mystified by the remark. Jack explained, "There's always going to be some hot investment that everybody's jumping on—real estate, tech or oil stocks, commodities, currency, gold—you name it. When some of your friends start bragging about the killing they're making, you may find yourself thinking you're missing out."

"I can see how talk like that could be unsettling," Katie said.

Jack went on, "A B.O.Y. plan is all about building a solid financial foundation and a secure future—you're not going to see those thrilling spikes. But you're also *not* going to have those unpredictable, heart-stopping losses that inevitably follow. And that's when you'll thank your lucky stars for your B.O.Y. plan. Besides, if an investment opportunity comes up that you want to take advantage of, you can do that by using equity from your B.O.Y. plan, and at least know you'll get the same guaranteed annual increase and dividends on the money you borrowed, even if the 'hot' investment doesn't pan out."

"B.O.Y. is about building a solid financial foundation and a secure future. You're not going to see those thrilling spikes, but you're also not going to have those unpredictable, heart-stopping losses that inevitably follow."

Katie looked at Paul and then said to Jack, "I think we've already had enough of those adrenaline rushes and crashes with our investments and financial plan to last us a lifetime. We're ready for a plan we can count on, right, honey?"

"Definitely. That's why we're here," agreed Paul. "We understand the three downsides and they're not a problem."

"Actually, I just thought of one more," Jack confessed. "Like your friend Rob, you're probably not going to want to keep B.O.Y. a secret from the people you know and care about. And you're going to find that frustrating at times."

"Why would it be frustrating?" Katie inquired.

"Because some people will be open-minded and decide to start B.O.Y. plans of their own. But others will argue with you and try to tell you why what you're doing doesn't make sense. And they'll stay the course—even when that course clearly isn't working for them—out of fear of taking another route. Even lab rats will go down a dead-end path in a maze only once or twice before giving up and trying a different way. Humans can waste a *lifetime* wandering down the same blind alley, refusing to even *try* going in another direction."

"Thanks for the warning, Jack," Paul said. "I guess we'll have to learn to live with that one."

"Is there some better way out there to do all these things?" Jack asked. "Maybe . . . but so far no one has walked away with the cash reward B.O.Y. is offering to anybody who can show they use a different financial product that has all the advantages and guarantees of Bank On Yourself."

"Yeah—Rob mentioned it to me. I told Katie about it before we came in to see you the first time," Paul said. "You know, Katie sometimes complains I'm slow to make up my mind about a purchase, like a big-screen TV or a new refrigerator, because I keep thinking of one more feature the model I'm looking at doesn't have. I've been going over the things we talked about last week, and I came in today with those same kinds of reservations. Especially about what people like Suze Orman and Dave Ramsey say about whole life insurance. But you know what? You've stepped up to the plate on every issue I came in with."

Katie patted her husband's hand and added, "Coming from my husband, that's a real compliment. You've answered all our concerns and we're ready to sign whatever papers you need. But before that, I want to ask about my sister, Julie. I've told her about Bank On Yourself, and she and her husband want to know more about it, but they live in Ohio.

"She was wondering if she should just try going to the financial advisor she and her husband have used for investment and planning advice and see if he knows how to set up a B.O.Y. plan. But it's pretty clear now that it would be a mistake to go to someone who probably doesn't know anything about how B.O.Y. policies work or how to use them to finance things yourself. What do you suggest for her?"

"You're right," Jack told her. "It takes most advisors a year or so of additional training to learn all the ins and outs of B.O.Y. But there's a referral service where she can be put in touch with a Bank On Yourself Authorized Advisor with advanced training in B.O.Y., and receive a free Bank On Yourself Analysis that would show her and her husband what a plan custom-designed for their goals and dreams could do for them."

"That would be great," Katie answered.

"No problem, then," Jack replied. "Tell her to go to this Web site, and she'll find everything she needs, including a free report that summarizes how B.O.Y. works." On a sheet of memo paper, he wrote, **www.BankOnYourselfFreeAnalysis.com** and handed the paper to Katie, who took it from him with a nod and a smile.

"She has a health issue. Will that be a problem?" Katie asked.

"Not necessarily. Sometimes people think they're uninsurable, but it turns out not to be the case. So it's best to talk to a B.O.Y. Advisor before counting yourself out. Also, when you take out a plan, the insurance doesn't have to be on you. As long as you own the policy, you control the money in the policy. But the life insurance can be on someone else you're closely connected to, like a spouse or one of your children or a business associate. So that's an option, if it turns out Julie really is uninsurable."

"Don't count yourself out due to your age, a health issue, or another reason. For a free report summarizing how B.O.Y. works, and to get a referral to a Bank On Yourself Authorized Advisor who can do a free analysis that will show you how you could benefit from a custom-tailored B.O.Y. plan, visit www.BankOnYourselfFreeAnalysis.com."

"Good," Katie said, and Paul added, "Okay. So how do we get started?"

"As I explained, you're going to start two plans—one for Katie, that you'll be funding at $750 a month, the other for you, Paul, at $1,000 a month. And you're going to be making the changes in your 401(k) contributions and your credit cards and so on that we talked about, so most of this money will just be shifted from other items in your monthly budget."

"Which was pretty neat," Katie said. "I really appreciated the advice you gave us on that."

"All part of my job," Jack said. "It'll just take a few minutes to fill out the applications."

"Let's do it," Paul said and, smiling at Katie, added, "You realize this means we're giving up those four fancy dinners from Rob, though. . . ."

"Yeah, I know," replied Katie. "But we're doing something really good for ourselves, so I'm fine with that."

CHAPTER 6

Looking Ahead

Two roads diverged in a wood, and I—
I took the one less traveled by, and that has
made all the difference.
—Robert Frost

Let's flip the calendar pages into the future so we can observe the journey of Paul and Katie as they take advantage of the opportunities and benefits that Bank On Yourself provides them—one year after they started their plan, and the years after that, all the way through to their retirement.

Here's how one version of their life's journey with Bank On Yourself could play out. (The projections that appear here are based on the 2008 dividends. Dividends are not guaranteed and are subject to change.)

Just weeks after Paul and Katie started their Bank On Yourself plans, Katie was already talking to friends who had taken the trip to Africa with one of the groups from their church. Even though Paul had long known this was a dream of hers, he marveled at how she threw herself into the research. Never much of a reader beyond *Time* magazine and *Entertainment Weekly*, she was suddenly bringing home armloads of books about Africa and missionary work, and she spent whole evenings making "to do" lists and watching movies set in Africa.

Paul offered to sit down with her and plan the finances. She surprised him by insisting that this was her project and she was going to handle all the planning herself. He was secretly pleased; she had grown up with a strong-willed father who didn't think women should make any decisions, and was gaining a confidence about financial matters that Paul hadn't seen before. He only learned by accident that she had been discussing the financial aspects of the trip with Jack Richards, their B.O.Y. Advisor.

At one of those meetings, held three months before she was due to leave, Jack reviewed the details with her. For the month she would be away, Katie would be using two weeks of vacation plus two weeks of unpaid leave of absence. She had made exacting calculations of the costs for airfare, wardrobe items for the climate in Ghana when she would be there—warm, humid, rainy, sticky—plus her food, housing, transportation, and incidentals. Katie was determined to pay for all this out of her own pocket, most of which would be tax deductible as a donation, rather than by raising donations or holding pie auctions, as others going on the trip were doing.

She'd also need to come up with enough money to help cover household expenses, in place of the income she'd be giving up to make the trip. She was nervous about the total—nearly $4,000. Did she really have enough cash value in her B.O.Y. plan to cover that much?

When she sat down with Jack, he relieved her anxiety by reassuring her that her plan by then—one year after starting it—had almost $7,500 of value that she could borrow. He also explained that her plan actually had more cash value than that, but to make sure a policy owner doesn't inadvertently borrow more money than is available, which could make the policy lapse, the insurance company keeps a small cushion of cash value in the policy.

Even after taking the loan, Katie would still have nearly $3,500 available as an emergency cash reserve. Together they worked out that, after she returned, she would repay the loan over a two-year period, at the rate of $183 a month. And at the end of the two-year payback period, Katie would have the cost of the trip back in her B.O.Y. plan.

Jack said, "Give me only a minute or two and we can fill out a simple form to request your policy loan. Do you want the company to mail you a check for it? Or would you prefer to have the money transferred directly into your checking account? That way the funds could be available to you within a couple of days."

She asked, "Taking a loan is as simple as that?"

"That's it," he told her. "It's *your* money. Remember that favorite saying of mine: you can do with it whatever you want, whenever you want. You don't have to fill out any credit applications or pledge your wedding ring as collateral."

> "When you want to take a policy loan, you
> fill out a simple request form. You're not at
> the mercy of banks or credit card
> companies. You can have the company
> send you a check or transfer the money
> directly into your checking account."

"It sure is nice not to be at the mercy of banks or credit card companies. Just have them transfer the money to my bank account." And then she added, "I know you're busy. I appreciate your finding time to meet with me like this."

"My work for you doesn't end with designing your plan, Katie," he told her. "Think of me as your permanent Bank On Yourself coach. I'll be having meetings like this with you and Paul right through the years. I'll show you as you go along how to use your policy to maximize the growth, and how to take full advantage of the tax laws. I'll help you make smart decisions every step of the way for the best possible long-term results."

"I remember you saying that," she said. "But I guess I didn't think about needing your advice all along the way."

"You know, there are so many variables with these policies. Even for an experienced life insurance agent and financial advisor like me, it still took almost a year of additional training to really grasp all the ins and outs of Bank On Yourself—designing the best plan for each client's needs, all the variables involved with using your equity in the plan to make it grow at the fastest clip possible, the most tax-efficient ways to take income at retirement, and all the rest. Leaving you to make all the decisions on your own would be like putting you in a sailboat for the first time, tossing you a compass and life jacket, and expecting you to figure out how to reach the coast of England all on your own."

"I get seasick," Katie told him.

"In that case maybe the sailboat is an even more appropriate example," Jack said, laughing.

At home that night, there was one part of Katie's financial planning for the trip that she was glad to share with Paul: her incredible feeling of being able to make this long-standing dream of hers come true without putting them in debt to a credit card company or a bank. "I have to pinch myself to make sure I'm not dreaming," she told him. And then she grinned. Paul actually turned off the Denver Nuggets game to listen to her. "I'll pay back the cost to my B.O.Y. plan and then have all that money to use all over again for another trip or whatever else I want."

"Yes, Katie—that's how it works," he said. She thought he sounded a little condescending, as if what he really wanted to say was, "I've been paying attention, I already *know* that's how it works." But she let it go and sat down beside him, picked up the remote, turned the game back on, and stayed there watching it with him. At the next time-out, he went to the kitchen and came back with a beer for each of them. He had even poured hers into a glass.

*   *   *

A few days after they had said goodbye at the airport, Paul was surprised to find an e-mail from Katie. The idea that the remote village the group was headed for had some way that e-mails could be sent out simply mystified him. After she had assured him that the trip, though very long, had gone okay and that the living accommodations were much more primitive than she'd imagined, her message continued:

> All of us lugged those heavy bags through airport security, and on
> and off buses and vans, to bring what seemed like thousands of over-
> the-counter medications, the headache pills, upset-stomach tablets,
> cold and sore-throat remedies, and the rest. But the lines of mothers
> and children who came to see us seemed to stretch into the forest.
> (At least, when they could be talked into forming lines.) The stash of
> pills quickly began to look as if it would run out in only a few days.

Later the same week, Paul got an e-mail that talked about "the happy faces of the children, grateful smiles of the mothers, the delight of shy youngsters when they see an image of themselves on the screen of a digital camera." Katie also wrote:

> What we're doing seems like so little to us but obviously seems to
> them like such a magical thing. On market day, we buy apples or or-
> anges and the children act as if they had appeared from a treasure

chest. One small piece of fruit earns an entire day of smiles and grateful hugs.

I'm so glad I was able to do this. Please give Jack a personal thanks from me.

When Paul met her at the airport on her return, he thought she looked tired, yet with a glow of contentment he had rarely seen.

*   *   *

On a brisk winter day near the end of the third year after the couple had started their B.O.Y. plans, just as Paul was about to head home from work, he received a call from Jack, who had kept track of the Harpers' goals and car purchases and knew Paul would be thinking about visits to the local dealerships to replace his almost-four-year-old Cadillac. Paul went into Jack's office a few days later to have a conversation about the car.

"You have more than enough cash value in your B.O.Y. plan to finance that new vehicle yourself," Jack told him.

"That's the best news I've heard all year. I won't be making car payments to someone else's finance company anymore. I'll be making them to my own B.O.Y. plan, which means I'll start getting back the cost of my cars, plus the interest I've been shelling out to others, right?"

"Absolutely. Those dollars will be lining *your* pocket, instead of someone else's. And if you're like most of my clients, you may be surprised to find yourself actually looking *forward* to making those payments."

By borrowing from a B.O.Y. policy to pay cash for cars and other big-ticket items and making loan payments back to the policy, you can get back the money you pay for those items and recapture interest you now pay to finance institutions.

"It's hard to imagine looking forward to making car payments. . . ." Paul laughed.

"You'll see what I mean. Now about your new car," Jack said, "any ideas about what you're interested in?"

"I'm going to stick with another Cadillac. That means I'm looking at another $40,000 car, less the $10,000 trade-in value I expect my current car will have."

"I'm guessing you've never paid cash for a car before."

"Frankly, I can't even imagine what it's like to walk into a car dealership and be able to pay cash. I think those dealership finance people must all be sent away to some camp for a six-month training course called 'How to make the customer squirm.' It wasn't any better when I was leasing. The lower monthly payment seemed like a better deal than financing, but every time, at the end of the lease, I got stuck for the extra miles I put on and every little ding on the body. And then it bothered me that I had nothing to show for all the money I'd spent, after turning the car in."

"I can practically guarantee you won't be squirming this time," Jack told him. "We've put together a little resource packet for our clients on how to buy a car at a great price without all the haggling and game playing. You'll put in fifteen or twenty minutes of research in advance. By the time you walk in, you'll know what you should be paying, exactly what to say to get the best price, and how to get the most money for your trade-in. And since you're not going to use dealer financing, you eliminate the worst games the dealerships play that most people never win and hate the most."

"For the first time in my life, I might actually enjoy this," Paul replied.

"You can find the car-buying resource packet online," Jack said. He jotted a note for Paul that read:

Car buyers' resource packet: **www.BankOnYourself.com**.

Paul said, "Fine—but hang on a second. I see from the policy statements I get every year how my cash value is picking up some steam. Wouldn't I be better off *not* using the policy to finance a car now? Wouldn't Katie and I have more cash value over the long run that way?"

"Paul, this is really going to surprise you, just as it does most of my clients, but when you use your policy to finance things and make the same monthly payment back to your plan that you would have had to make to a finance company, your cash value can actually grow faster than if you *didn't* use it to finance things yourself!"

"Whoa," Paul said. "Did you really say what I thought you just said?"

Jack laughed. "Doesn't sound possible, right? I've gotten that reaction so often that it's no surprise anymore. So let me explain how that works. If you borrow $30,000 now to finance your next car yourself and pay the loan back the way I'll show you in a moment, and assuming you *never* use your policy again to finance another car, or anything else, for that matter, when you reach age sixty-five, you could have about $10,000 *more* cash value than if you'd never used your plan to finance anything!"

"Incredible," Paul said. "Just incredible. So if I *don't* use my plan to finance things, I'm not doing myself any favors."

"Exactly. You don't slow down the growth of your plan by using it this way to buy things, like you would if you took a 401(k) loan or used money you put in a savings or investment account. In fact, although it seems to defy logic, the more you borrow from your plan and make regular repayments back into it, the more wealth you could have."

Jack chuckled. Paul asked, "What's so funny?"

"I'm just thinking about my older brother, Mark," Jack answered. "I was never able to convince him about Bank On Yourself. Maybe it's because of the sibling rivalry we've always had. I think he figures that if he didn't come up with the idea, it couldn't be any good. But he liked the idea of letting *me* finance his cars, instead of using a finance company. So I borrowed the money I loaned my brother from my Bank On Yourself plan, and he's paying me back. Which means *I'm* now making the profits the finance company was making on him. Well, it's worked out fine. He's made every payment on time."

"Sounds like you got the last laugh on that deal," Paul grinned.

"Meanwhile," Jack went on, "I'm still getting my guaranteed annual cash value increase and the same dividends, even on the amount I loaned to him, so my capital is working for me in two different ways at the same time. To tell you the truth, I feel as if I'm taking advantage of him, but he's happy with the arrangement, and so am I."

"If I ever meet your brother, I'll try to remember not to chuckle!" Paul said.

Jack told him, "Ya know what's fun? When the cocktail-party or water-cooler conversation turns to who negotiated the best deal on their latest car. You know how it seems like there's always someone who manages to negotiate a better car deal than you? Well, wait till you see the looks of awe and envy on their faces when you tell them you got the best deal of all—because you're getting back every penny you paid for your car and *then* some."

"I'm looking forward to that," Paul said with a mischievous smile.

"Okay," said Jack. "Let's get you started. I always advise my clients to set up their loan repayment schedule at the same time they take their loan, because unlike borrowing from a finance company, the insurance company isn't going to require you to pay back a certain amount each month, or even make you pay your loan back. That's up to you, and to make it really simple, I recommend you have the loan repayments automatically deducted from your checking account every month. It's easy to set that up at the same time you request your loan."

It's a good idea to set up a loan repayment schedule at the same time that you take a policy loan. It's simple to do and you can choose to have the payments automatically deducted from your checking account.

"Great. Automatic means one less thing to think about," Paul said. After a moment, he asked, "But if I do that, what happens if I have a temporary cash crunch and I need that money for a medical bill or whatever?"

"Then we just contact the company and have them stop the automatic deduction. What's great is that you *can* do that, if you need to. It's not like when you use a credit card or a bank loan. You won't even incur any late fees, and nobody is going to annoy you with collection calls or send a goon squad to repossess your car. You won't get a ding on your credit report, either."

"So—nobody's going to get on my back if I need to skip payments for a while?"

Jack grinned and shook his head. "Not exactly," he said. "*I'll* be on your back. I won't be harassing you, of course, but keeping after you to get back to your regular payments as soon as you can. Sometimes people think, 'Hey—it's my money, I can do whatever I want.' And that's true, but by not consistently paying yourself back, you'd be losing out on a lot of the wealth-building power of Bank On Yourself."

"So how do I figure out the amount I should be setting my monthly payment at?" Paul asked.

"Let me walk you through that. When you take a policy loan, the insurance company charges you interest, of course—at a very reasonable rate."

"So the amount I pay back every month needs to cover the interest as well. I get that," Paul said. "And the interest shows up as a credit—an increase in the value of my plan?"

"Yes and no. It ultimately benefits you, but it doesn't go directly into your policy. Do you remember when we talked about how when you borrow against your cash value, the money doesn't actually come directly from your policy?"

"Yes. You said it comes from the company's general fund, because all the cash value in all the policies is pooled together," Paul responded.

"Exactly. And it works the same way in the opposite direction: the payments you make on your loan don't go back directly into your policy, they go where they came from—back into the company's general fund. The company applies your payments of principal to reduce your loan balance. Then, at the end of each year, the company looks at their income from all sources, including the loan interest you paid, and they look at their expenses and the death claims they paid out. As long as their results are better than the worst-case scenario they projected, they pay a dividend to all the policy owners."

Paul interjected, "Since the company you put me with hasn't missed paying dividends in a century, I'm not planning to spend much time worrying over whether they're going to miss in the next few years."

Jack smiled and said, "No question that's a great track record. But no matter what happens in the future, you don't have to worry about getting your preset, guaranteed cash value increases each year. Those are automatic."

"So even though the interest I pay on my loans doesn't go directly into my policy, I eventually get the benefit, along with all the other policyholders, through a combination of the guaranteed annual increases, plus any dividends the company pays. Is that it?"

> Policy loans come from the company's
> general fund, because the cash value in all
> the policies is pooled together. Interest
> paid on loans goes back to the general
> fund, and the policyholder ultimately gets
> the benefit through a combination of
> guaranteed annual increases, plus any
> dividends the company pays.

"You got it," Jack replied. "What's important is that you're *way* better off than paying interest to a bank, credit card, or finance company and saying goodbye to both your principal and interest. Or paying cash and giving up the interest and income you *could* have been getting on your money. The long and short of it is that both the principal and interest you pay ultimately end up in your B.O.Y. plan for you to use over and over again—for another car, a boat, a home theater, home repairs, or whatever you want."

"I can't *wait* to have that happen with my next car," Paul said. "Thanks for explaining what happens with the interest I pay on my policy loans. So let's get back to how to calculate what my monthly loan repayment to my plan should be. . . ."

"You *could* just pay back the loan at the interest rate the company is charging," Jack explained. "That's about 6 percent now. For a $30,000 loan over four years, that would make your monthly payment around $705. If you do that, your plan will grow nicely, and you'll end up with the *same* growth as you would if you didn't use your plan to finance things. But it won't grow as fast as it *could*. So let's look at it another way."

"I think maybe I see where you're heading. Am I allowed to pay something extra each month? Is that what you're suggesting I do?" Paul asked.

Jack beamed. "Yes! Right on target. You're allowed to pay extra. And, yes, that's what I'm suggesting. You see, any time you run a major purchase through your B.O.Y. plan and pay it back at the interest rate the company is charging, rather than financing, leasing, or paying cash for it, you're using the Spend and Grow Wealthy method. But there's an interesting variation we like to use that can result in significantly more wealth for you. We call this the Spend and Grow Even Wealthier way to buy big-ticket items."

"It sounds intriguing. How does that work?" Paul asked.

"I designed your B.O.Y. plan so that if you pay a little extra on top of the interest you're being charged, the company will treat that extra amount as additional dollars going into your paid-up additions rider. We've talked about that before."

"I remember about the PUAR. But I'm not sure I understand where you're going with this."

"The current car-loan rate finance companies charge is about 7.5 percent. On a $30,000, four-year loan, that would make your payments $725 a month. That's how much you were going to pay if you financed your next car the way you've done it in the past. That's twenty bucks more than what your monthly payment would be if you just paid it back at the interest rate the company's charging, and that extra would go into your PUAR. But I'd like to suggest you tack on just a little bit more than that," Jack explained.

"How much more were you going to suggest?" Paul asked.

Jack replied, "Could you handle a total monthly payment of $750? That's only $25 more a month than you were going to pay the finance company."

"No sweat. I don't think I'd even notice the extra $25."

"Good," Jack continued. "Remember when I said that the PUAR is like putting your policy on legal steroids—it really turbo charges the growth of your cash value? Any extra dollars that go into your PUAR will really light a fire under your cash value. *That's* what we mean when we talk about the B.O.Y. Spend and Grow Even Wealthier way to buy things. You can end up with a lot more wealth without having to make risky investments. And you can enjoy more of life's luxuries without the guilt."

By using the B.O.Y. Spend and Grow
Even Wealthier way to buy things,
you can end up with more wealth
without making risky investments
and you can enjoy more of life's
luxuries without guilt.

"You know something?" Paul said. "It really makes you think about money and financing in a whole different way. If more people knew about this, our country wouldn't be in the situation we're in—people in debt up to their ears, looking to depend on totally unpredictable stock and real estate markets and on Social Security and Medicare for money that probably won't be there. And there wouldn't be a retirement crisis either."

Jack grinned—amused that if anyone had been eavesdropping just then, they might have thought Paul was the advisor and Jack the client.

*   *   *

A few weeks later, with $30,000 from the insurance company in his checking account, Paul walked into the dealership, accompanied by Katie. For once he didn't feel as if he was going to be embarrassed and intimidated, pressured about options and extras he didn't need or want. And he definitely knew he wasn't going to get jerked around by the finance department.

This time it was a snap. Paul had in hand a list of all the options he wanted and was armed with the research he'd done at Jack's suggestion, along with a printout of what he could expect to get for his trade-in. They both sensed their salesman wasn't very happy, especially since a customer who pays cash for his car means the dealership won't collect all the extra money it would otherwise get for writing a car loan. But Paul and Katie knew they were in charge. And they knew there were other Cadillac dealerships in town they could go to if they didn't like the way they were being treated.

They walked out feeling so elated about how painless it was, and what a great deal they were able to negotiate, that they decided to splurge on dinner at one of Katie's favorite restaurants.

Over dinner they decided they would call Jack the next morning and start their third B.O.Y. plan so they could finance all of Katie's cars the same way. And in the process, they would be adding still more to their retirement fund, money they knew they could predict and count on.

*   *   *

When Katie got home from her meeting with Jack about her new plan, she told Paul, "You know what, honey? I'm really glad I kept up with paying my plan back for the Africa trip and the other loan I took to cover what it cost us when I had to help my father after his surgery. I'm all caught up now. I've paid my plan back for both the loans."

"That's good news," Paul said.

"Wait, wait. You haven't heard the *really* good news yet." Flinging her arms around his neck, she said, "That B.O.Y. plan of mine now has way more than enough cash value in it to go on our dream trip to Paris!"

They had hardly started their planning before they realized they weren't going to have to make it a no-frills trip. They understood that they'd be able to save for retirement *and* enjoy the good things in life. Simply by paying for luxuries using their Bank On Yourself plans, and then paying the money back, they would be able to enjoy living well, guilt free—because they wouldn't be missing a single beat in financing their retirement.

Paris didn't turn out to be what they had imagined; it turned out to be vastly better—it was magical, with memorable sights everywhere they looked, from the architecture of ancient buildings, to the oh-so-French atmosphere of the streets, to the romance of the sidewalk cafés, to the lights of the city at night. Everything was so steeped in history that it almost felt like a trip back in time. The challenge for Katie had been whether to take a weeklong cooking class and have only a couple of days for sightseeing, or take a one-day class and be a tourist for most of their stay.

She decided to take the one-day class at the International Kitchen, and eat great food rather than spend more days cooking it. They had dinner one night at the three-star Benoît, for as much money as they usually spent on three months of eating out, but they agreed it was worth every euro. And they had fabulous meals at little restaurants and cafés that they picked at random.

They saw the Eiffel Tower, Notre Dame Cathedral, and the Arc de Triomphe, went to the Louvre and the wonderful Musée d'Orsay (which they liked even better), and took an unforgettable nighttime boat ride on the Seine. They came home exhausted, but both feeling changed, exhilarated, and eager for more travel.

When they dropped by to see Jack, they were armed with a selection of photos for him to choose from for his wall. And they were already talking about where they would go next. Katie's B.O.Y. plan by then was already growing fast enough that they realized they'd be able to take their next dream trip in only another two years. "And," Jack told them, "you should be able to take off for a new destination every couple of years until you run out of places you want to go."

To Paul, Katie looked as happy as she had been on her wedding day.

*   *   *

Though the trip to Paris was the experience of a lifetime for Katie and Paul, coming back to Denver didn't turn out to be as happy. They'd been back less than two weeks when Katie's father, in Minneapolis, took a bad fall and had to be moved into an assisted-living facility. Katie flew back home twice to help her sister sort through the lifetime collection of items and decide what to dispose of. The cost of the trips, and the additional time away from work, put an unexpected crunch on their cash flow.

She and Paul discussed the situation with Jack. "It's at times like this that the flexibility you have with Bank On Yourself plans can be a real lifesaver," he told them. "You have several options you can fall back on to get through a cash-flow crunch like this."

Katie relaxed into her chair as Jack continued, "You could skip paying back the policy loan you took for your trip to Paris for a while, or you could take another policy loan from your plan or Paul's plan and not count on repaying it right away. Or you could scale back or skip the paid-up additions rider portion of your premium payment for a while. Or you could do a combination."

Jack explained that he had set up their B.O.Y. policies with a company that offered a very flexible paid-up additions rider. "You're allowed to put in all, some, or none of the full amount of the rider every year. I know you're committed to putting in the full amount so your plan will grow as fast as possible, but when cash flow is a problem, the company allows you to make up the difference in future years."

> If an emergency comes up or you have
> a cash-flow crunch, a B.O.Y. plan gives
> you flexibility to skip some loan
> repayments. Some companies offer
> a flexible PUAR, which allows you to
> put in all, some, or none of the full
> amount of the rider each year.

After discussing their options, the couple agreed that they would stop paying back the loan they'd taken for the Paris trip until their financial situation improved. Jack explained that if they didn't repay an amount during any year at least equal to the interest due on the loan, the insurance company would simply deduct the interest from their cash value at the end of the policy year.

Katie looked at her husband. "And let's take another policy loan to pay back the costs of my trips to Minneapolis. I put it on a credit card, but by transferring the cost into our B.O.Y. plans, we'll get the cost of the trips and the interest back." To Jack she said, "You can't even imagine what a relief this is."

"Actually, I can," Jack said. "And it's not just that I've been through this with a number of clients before you. There was a time when I had to do the same thing myself, taking multiple loans and holding off on repaying loans I'd already taken from my own policies."

Katie looked at him with new eyes. "I guess that makes us members of the same club," she said.

*   *   *

In the years that followed, Katie and Paul made trips to Tuscany, Hong Kong, Thailand, Brazil, and Tokyo. As their incomes grew, they started additional B.O.Y. policies, eventually owning seven between them. And along the way they decided to stop funding their 401(k)s altogether, due to poor and unpredictable performance, and the fact that both their employers had stopped matching contributions.

On one of their regular visits with Jack, he told them that the first of their plans had reached the point where the premiums could be paid "internally." This meant, he explained, that the dividends in their plan could be sufficient to be used to pay future premiums.

* * *

Shortly after Paul's fifty-eighth birthday, he passed out in the middle of a meeting at work and was rushed to the hospital. It turned out to be a heart problem; Paul, who had been as healthy and fit as any man they knew in his age group, underwent triple bypass surgery.

As if that weren't scary enough, after the surgery they received medical bills—from the doctors and physical therapists, the anesthesiologist, and the hospital—totaling more than $22,000. That's how much Paul was responsible for, after his company health plan had paid its share. "The deductible, copayment, and noncovered items," they were told by way of explanation.

Twenty-two thousand dollars! They learned that unexpected medical expenses cause 50 percent of bankruptcies and that 75 percent of those folks had health insurance at the time.

Even though it hurt, Paul actually managed a laugh when he found out that they needed to come up with $22,000. Katie was baffled by his reaction. "We'll just borrow it from one of our Bank On Yourself plans," he told her. "Imagine what it would have meant if we didn't have Bank On Yourself and had to take the money out of our 401(k)s or put it on credit cards."

A B.O.Y. plan can provide a cash cushion to help you weather unexpected medical expenses, disability, job loss, or other emergency.

Just two years later, Paul had paid back the loan to his B.O.Y. plan. He bragged to Katie, "We actually made a 'profit' on the medical bills for my surgery! How many people do you think can say that?"

* * *

Paul and Katie retired the year they both turned sixty-eight, as they had planned all along. Because they had been faithful through the years about paying back all the policy loans the B.O.Y. Spend and Grow Even Wealthier way—adding a little extra to each payment to go into the PUAR—the combined total of their seven Bank On Yourself plans turned out to be just as good as Jack had originally projected. Even after spending for the foreign travel, the new cars every four years for each of them, and Paul's surgery bills, they were, as the saying goes, sitting pretty.

Though the value of their B.O.Y. plans turned out fairly close to what had been predicted, they still found the numbers astounding. On more or less average incomes, the total amount they could access by the time they retired at sixty-eight had reached close to $1.25 million, *just* from the first two of the seven B.O.Y. plans they had started. Those were the plans they had funded primarily by redirecting money they had been contributing to the 401(k) plans they felt they couldn't count on into B.O.Y. plans that they knew they could.

And all along, they both had the comfort of knowing that if either one of them died, the other would receive the full current death benefit of the policy, less any outstanding loans. The added peace of mind and the freedom to fully enjoy their retirement felt like a blessing.

Living to age ninety and beyond had become common, and Jack had always insisted Paul and Katie plan their finances as though they would live to be one hundred. That meant they were able to take a retirement income of around $70,000 a year, just from their first two B.O.Y. plans, for a total of $2.31 million over those thirty-three years of retirement, because their plans continued to grow while they were taking income.

Primarily by redirecting money they had been contributing to the 401(k) plans they couldn't count on into B.O.Y. plans they knew they could, Paul and Katie could have $2.31 million of retirement income.

Looking back, they were very grateful that Paul had taken Rob up on that bet all those years ago.

* * *

This story of Paul and Katie paints a picture of what life might be like for one couple who embrace Bank On Yourself.

In the chapters that follow, you'll meet real folks from all walks of life who have agreed to share real-life stories of their own personal Bank On Yourself journeys.

PART THREE

Real People, Real Experiences

Probably the most effective way to help you understand the impact Bank On Yourself has on the lives of people of all ages, incomes, and backgrounds is to let some of these folks tell you their personal stories in their own words.

It's astonishing how many different ways there are for people to use B.O.Y. to reach a variety of short- and long-term personal and financial goals and dreams, and how those dreams can come true in a surprisingly short period of time. The possibilities are limited only by one's imagination.

The people who agreed to share their stories in the pages that follow revealed many personal and intimate details of their finances, family, and upbringing. Some understandably requested that I not reveal their identity, and in those cases I have used fictitious names and changed a few identifying details to preserve their privacy.

Each person I interviewed was joined by their Bank On Yourself Authorized Advisor, who helped fill in some of the details and numbers. However, out of fairness to the other two hundred–some B.O.Y. Advisors, those who took part in the interviews that follow are not identified by name.

CHAPTER 7

Building a Comfortable Retirement You Can Predict and Count On

Some people don't seem to mind the uncertainty and unpredictability of traditional strategies for investing and retirement planning. Others want to be able to know their nest egg will be there when they're ready to retire, and that's a key benefit many B.O.Y. clients mention as a hot button.

The experience of an Ohio family is an inspiring example of how B.O.Y. can help people reach both their long- and short-term financial and lifestyle goals, while financing a secure retirement at the same time.

How a Dog Bite Landed One Family on the Fast Track to Financial Security

Christy and Greg Gammon are real estate entrepreneurs and the parents of two teenagers. The setting for the interview was the vacation beach home where they were married, not far from where the Wright Brothers made the world's first airplane flight. The home looks out onto the ocean. Greg set the scene with this description: "The waves are crashing in. The seagulls are soaring on the wind and the sand is blowing around. We're looking at God's creation and just marveling at this beauty. There is nothing quite like the Outer Banks of North Carolina."

He went on by giving his own personal description of his wife: "Christy is a petite five-foot-two. Brown hair, beautiful brown eyes. She takes care of herself and is just a beautiful woman." She responded with her description of him: "Greg is the epitome of tall, dark, and handsome. He's about six-foot-three. He's now moved on to salt-and-pepper hair, which I think suggests a wisdom about him. He's just very attractive inside and out."

The story of how they came to learn about Bank On Yourself is amusingly convoluted.

Christy:

We were about to buy our first home together, and we had a little dog who got himself into some trouble, biting a neighbor. We took the little girl to the hospital. When our insurance company found out that our dog had bitten someone, they dropped us. So with just two or three days to go until our closing, we had to find new insurance.

Greg jumped online and found the cheapest homeowners' insurance he could. He said, "At least this will get us through closing." When we sat down with the insurance agent to go through the policy, he said, "I understand you're here to just get this done today, but I'd really like you to meet my partner. We've got some exciting things that we think might be appropriate for you."

So, of course, we were just kind of rolling our eyes and said, "We've got to get out of here and get done what we need to get done." But we never forgot that meeting, and we did get back with them.

One of the partners was a B.O.Y. Advisor, and that's what they wanted to tell the Gammons about.

Greg:

They handed us some material to read. I read it and my response was probably a typical response many people might have. "This sounds good, but does it really work?" We talked more about the Bank On Yourself idea, and that's essentially how we got started.

At the time I saw it as a way to accumulate some money and not have to worry about dealing with banks in terms of "Will our credit hold up? And what if we run into a situation where we need to skip a loan payment or two?"

From that standpoint, I was looking at it as a way to just get away from having to deal with banks, whether it was for business or personal use.

We were starting to get more involved in real estate and looking into going into business for ourselves.

The premium on our first policy was going to be $1,000 a month. As we talked with the B.O.Y. specialist, he gave us some ideas on how we could reduce our discretionary spending and be a little more disciplined in terms of how we spend our money on personal expenses.

So we went through a financial analysis with him and realized, "Here's some money that we can free up." The first thing we changed is we didn't eat out as much. We had a lot more meals at home, and that saved us a couple hundred dollars a month, surprisingly.

It actually felt really good, because we felt like we were making the best decisions for our family. We knew it was going to enable us to make some life changes that were very important to us.

Christy:

We also talked to our phone company and had our Internet, phone, and cable all bundled, so we got a much better rate on those. Fundamentally we started to view the policy as our savings. We had already been putting money into a more traditional savings account.

If you can free your mind of what people conventionally do and put those funds into your policy instead of a bank like everyone else, then the value builds faster.

The $1,000 a month was a little bit daunting at first because that's a lot of money to us, but we've been very consistent with it.

For the Gammons, one of the greatest values of Bank On Yourself has nothing to do with finances. Because it has allowed them to leave their 9-to-5 jobs and carve independent careers working together, the independence has brought an unexpected blessing.

Christy:

One thing that this has given us is the flexibility in our time. It's not necessarily the "Oh, we took this vacation during that year" but just the day-to-day things, like being more involved in our teenage sons' lives and being able to pick up our boys from school.

We first started doing that about four or five years ago. Picture
Zach at age eleven. He's got soccer and homework. Just to be able to
have either Greg or me pick him up after school each day, and fix
him a snack and solve some of the world's problems and get his
homework done—those are times that are so precious to me. And if I
were working an 8-to-5 job, which usually lasts until 8 p.m., I would
have been robbed of those times. That's what I will never regret.

Greg:

I think a lot of people realize that too late in life. We were able to realize it before it was too late.

So now we have some really very powerful memories because of
the lifestyle changes that we made, the things that we've done as a
family because we had the good counsel of our B.O.Y. Advisor.
B.O.Y. has given us the freedom to do these things that were ultimately more important than anything else that we would have spent
our money on.

> "B.O.Y. has given us flexibility in our time to
> be more involved in our teenage sons' lives
> and the freedom to do those things that
> are ultimately more important than
> anything we could have spent our
> money on."

And I can tell you that more than once both boys have said, "We really appreciate that you're there for us." There is nothing like that as
a parent, hearing that from your child.

Christy:

Our main goal for the children was to set up funding for their college educations. Our oldest son just turned eighteen, and the other
one is fifteen. As it turns out our oldest son, who would have triggered our first withdrawals here in the fall as he starts college, has

joined the Reserves of the Marines, so they are going to be taking
care of a large percentage of his college funding.

Greg and Christy didn't stop with their first B.O.Y. plan. As
Christy explained:

> We started a second policy shortly after the first one, and the total
> premium is $20,000 a year. We had an inheritance when Greg's
> stepfather passed away, so we took a large chunk of that money and
> started this policy.
>
> The base portion of the premium is about $850 a month, or
> around $10,000 a year. The rest was for the paid-up additions
> rider—the part of the premium that really makes the cash value
> grow very quickly.

The Gammons appreciated the flexibility of their B.O.Y.-designed
policy. They used the windfall they'd received to pay both the base
premium and the paid-up additions rider premium the first year.
Then, for cash-flow reasons, because paying the PUAR is optional,
they went back down to paying only the base amount of $850 a
month.

Not very many insurance companies offer this rider, even though
it's of very high value to the policy owner. Some companies also allow
the paid-up additions rider to be flexible so that if the family hits a period when cash flow is tight, the portion of the premium that goes to
the PUAR doesn't have to be paid but can be made up later on as
finances improve. This flexibility is a powerful feature—as everyone
who has ever felt the pinch of sudden illness or unexpected medical
expenses or the loss of a job knows too well.

That means they're giving up the faster growth of cash value during
that period; they'll want to start paying again as soon as they're in a
position to.

Only a handful of companies allow a policyholder to make up for
PUAR premiums they may have missed in previous years, and the
Gammons' plan was written through one of those companies. In addition, some companies allow clients to pay the PUAR portion only as
an annual payment. The company used for the Gammons' plan gives
policyholders a choice of paying it monthly, quarterly, semiannually,

or annually, and the policyholder can change the payment frequency anytime he or she wants.

They've also started two other policies, one for each of their boys, for a total of four so far.

Greg and Christy have clear goals for the lifestyle they want to have when they retire. For them it's the difference between needs and wants.

Christy:

We've completely changed our perspective on what our employment is. I see it in stark contrast to someone like my father, who has punched a clock and paid his dues, and he's literally counting down the days until he retires.

I don't really think that way anymore. I enjoy our life, and we enjoy our work together, so I'm not focused on "Okay, when do I get to quit?" Because I don't necessarily want to.

Greg and I have done some missionary work and have realized that to simplify is what's best for us. You just look at the world around you and realize the difference between needs and wants. We have a certain size house right now and two cars and things like that, because we think that's what's necessary when you have children. But we're looking forward to downsizing within the next three years.

Greg:

I think quite honestly we're satisfied with what we are working toward as far as an income once we hit retirement age.

The Gammons' Christian values came through during our interview, and I was left with a sense that that had given them the strength to do some of the things that have turned their lives around. When I suggested that, Greg said, "Right. A lot of faith." And Christy added, "It gives us the strength to do everything that we do."

And what of that dog bite that led them to B.O.Y.? "It was divine intervention," they both agreed.

* * *

The Retirement Plan Alternative

Dick Nelson, a computer analyst in the aerospace industry, was intrigued by B.O.Y. because he wanted a secure retirement and realized it could give him advantages his traditional company retirement plan did not.

Dick:

I have a really fun job that I like—I get to play with all the new software. But my wife, Donna, is a nurse. She wants to quit because she has to work so hard. I met her in high school and went out with her on a bet. We have four children, grown and married, and doing very well on their own.

I grew up in a small town in western Washington. There was a lot of financial pressure on my parents. We always had what we needed, if not necessarily what we wanted. We never went hungry, but there was always that undertone of needing to work really hard. I remember my dad had two jobs at one time because he wasn't making enough money as a policeman, so he also drove a big truck for a transport company.

To help paint a picture for you, Dick described himself as five-foot-eight with a gray beard, glasses, and "a space between my two front teeth," and his wife, Donna, is the same height, with brown hair and blue eyes. It was Donna who encouraged him to look into Bank On Yourself. Dick explained how that came about.

My wife usually has a radio on at night. I think she does that so she doesn't have to hear me. Every once in a while I see her get up in the dark and write something down. One night she heard about Bank On Yourself. The next morning she said, "Hey, check this out; it sounds interesting." So I went onto the Web site and read about it, and it sounded really interesting to me, too.

It made a lot of sense, and it fit in with my philosophy.

I had been borrowing money from my company retirement plan account and paying it back. I don't like paying interest, so I figured that if I was going to pay interest, I was going to pay it to myself. What really interested me about B.O.Y. was that

when I borrowed from my company retirement account, the
money I borrowed would only grow by the interest I paid back
in on my loan, while a B.O.Y. plan would continue to grow as
though I hadn't taken a loan. It was something that was very
logical to me.

Dick requested a referral to an experienced B.O.Y. Advisor, who
worked with him to answer his questions, gather information about
his situation, and put together a custom-tailored plan. At the outset,
Dick tapped a money source he already had available.

I'm using money out of my retirement account to fund my Bank
On Yourself policy. I want to be able to more or less guarantee to
my wife how much money she will have on a continuing basis for a
long time, because I don't know if I will live to be old, but I expect
she will.
   I like the idea of having a guaranteed income coming for a
specific length of time. I was principally looking for a secure retirement. That was the main attraction of Bank On Yourself for me.

"The main attraction of Bank On Yourself
for me is having a guaranteed income
coming in for a specific length of time. I
was principally looking for a secure
retirement."

As we saw earlier, Americans typically spend hundreds of thousands
of dollars on cars during their lifetime. When you consider that the
median amount preretirees have accumulated in retirement accounts
is only $81,000 (according to the Federal Reserve Board's latest avail-
able [2007] Survey of Consumer Finances), simply recapturing the
money spent on cars by financing those purchases through a Bank On
Yourself plan could provide many people with a retirement fund
many times larger than they would have otherwise.
   Dick Nelson had already figured out that buying cars for cash and
paying the interest to himself beat paying interest to a finance or leasing company.

I had bought two cars by borrowing from my company retirement account. Of course, you had to sell the underlying investments to come up with the cash. With a Bank On Yourself plan, you never have to sell any assets or investments.

And B.O.Y. is nice because I'm still collecting the guaranteed annual cash value increase, plus dividends on the money I've borrowed. I wasn't earning anything on the money I'd taken out of my company retirement plan. With B.O.Y., all of your money is still working for you.

I was really proud of myself when we started taking loans from the Bank On Yourself policy. Now every time I think about it, I get this big grin on my face.

For Dick, besides the realization that B.O.Y. was an even better way to finance major purchases, there was another, even stronger reason for not wanting to take additional car loans from his retirement plan at work.

I was getting to the point where I didn't want to have another loan on that account, because when I retire, I'd have to pay it back, so I financed our last couple cars through a bank.

How Dick and his wife are paying for travel has also changed drastically.

What we did last year was use credit cards to keep us going while Donna was traveling. Our youngest son is in Ohio, and he and his wife are both doctors in the Air Force. Donna is going back there to visit them. She did this twice last year because he's being deployed for a few weeks, and his wife is working twelve- to fourteen-hour days, and they have a baby.

So Donna is going back to Ohio soon for a couple weeks, and when she comes back we're going to Hawaii for two weeks. She doesn't have any vacation time, so she won't get paid anything during that month off.

Since Dick had recently taken a $45,000 loan from his B.O.Y. policy and had used part of it to pay off loans on a car and a truck, he

decided he would simply hold off making car loan repayments to his
B.O.Y. plan for two or three months. Not having to make those car
payments gave Dick and Donna breathing room and a cash cushion
they could use to help cover living expenses during the month Donna
would have no income, as well as covering the cost of Donna's trip.
They wouldn't have to use their credit cards for these expenses, as they
had in the past.

> The thing that really interested me was the fact that people have
> been doing this for over a hundred years. This isn't something
> new—rich people have been doing it forever.

Bank On Yourself, Dick said, "is a way for ordinary people to be
able to behave like rich people and use their money smart."

> So many people these days are using the money that *could* have gone
> to fund their retirement to pay for cars or to pay for their kids' col-
> lege. That's a big chunk of change.

With five years left until he planned to retire, Dick explained he
had cut back on what he was paying into his company's retirement
plan to the level his employer matched. And he was drawing down
that plan over a five-year period and moving the money into his
B.O.Y. plan. Though Dick pays income taxes on those withdrawals,
because he's sixty-one, he doesn't have to pay the 10 percent
premature-distribution penalty. Did Dick mind paying income taxes
on the money he was withdrawing from his company plan to move
into his B.O.Y. plan? I got my answer when I asked him how much
he expects to have to live on in retirement:

> The number in my mind is about $8,000 a month. I think actually
> it's going to be better because that target was what I had with my
> company plan, and I really feel that the Bank On Yourself plan is
> going to give us more. It's a better way and you don't have that un-
> certainty about your future.

Of course, money from his B.O.Y. plan is income he'll be able to
take without any taxes due on it, if the tax laws don't change.

I asked Dick how his life might have been different if he'd discovered B.O.Y. ten years earlier.

> My gosh! I think of all that money we've spent on cars and remodeling, plus all the interest we've paid. *I'd probably have been retired five years ago!*

As we wrapped up the interview, Dick mentioned how useful our conversation had been to him. That got me curious, so I asked about that statement. He answered:

> It reinforced this for me. You know, sometimes you go off and do something and then you forget all the good reasons why. It makes me want to go out and start another B.O.Y. plan!

To which Dick's B.O.Y. Advisor responded by saying he'd see if he could squeeze Dick into his busy schedule.

* * *

Oops! You Retired Too Young and Can't Get Your Hands on Your Retirement Funds

Tom Snyder, who grew up in Bucks County, Pennsylvania, worked for years as a telephone lineman.

> I started when I was eighteen. My last job was what they call an outside plant technician. I ran the wires, cables, and stuff like that for Verizon Communications.

Tom found out the hard way the problems and restrictions of government-sponsored retirement plans like 401(k)s and IRAs. He retired after thirty years at the company, but he wasn't even fifty years old, which meant that he couldn't take an income from his 401(k) plan without either paying early withdrawal penalties or jumping through restrictive hoops to get his hands on his own money.

When I spoke with Tom, he was fifty-four, still young enough that he had taken another job. To be able to pull money out of the 401(k) he had from his days at Verizon, he had done something known as a 72(t). This is a reference to a section of the IRS tax code that provides a way for people who haven't yet turned fifty-nine and a half to take withdrawals from a 401(k) or IRA without having it considered a premature distribution that would require a 10 percent penalty.

One of the drawbacks to a 72(t) is that you have to take equal distributions for a minimum of five years or until age fifty-nine and a half, whichever is longer. The specific amount you must withdraw each year is based on how long you're expected to live. Tom explained his frustration:

> I'm limited by the 72(t) as to how much I can pull out for the next five years. I would probably pull more out than I'm doing now, if I could.
>
> My biggest complaint I have is I didn't hear about Bank On Yourself earlier. I can tell you exactly what would have been different. The company matched 6 percent of the 401(k). I would have put just that percentage in, and the rest would have gone into a B.O.Y. policy. I wouldn't have been taxed to death, and I wouldn't be in this situation where I have all this money I can't touch right now because I'm only fifty-four. That would be the difference.
>
> I'm sure if I'd done my homework, I would have known about these traditional retirement plan restrictions. But who's thinking about retirement at eighteen years old?

"I'm sure if I'd done my homework, I would have known about the restrictions that traditional retirement plans have. But who's thinking about retirement at eighteen years old? My biggest complaint is that I didn't hear about B.O.Y. earlier."

There is a sad chapter to Tom's story. One of his four children, his son Tommy, died in a motorcycle accident a little over two years before our conversation.

The pain hasn't gone away yet. It won't ever go away, I don't think. Our lives have changed forever, but we're surviving, and that's what matters.

People don't generally buy Bank On Yourself policies primarily for the death benefit, but sometimes life throws you a curveball. When Tom was setting up his first policy, he thought about what it could mean for his children if they started with Bank On Yourself while still young.

At a meeting with my B.O.Y. Advisor, which was the fall of 2004, we were talking about my son Tommy, and I asked, "Tommy is making pretty good money. Do you think you might be able to help him?"

Tom's advisor picked up the story:

Tommy was in his twenties, an age people aren't typically thinking too much about their financial future, and when the father asked about a plan for Tommy, I suggested he give his son some information about Bank On Yourself. I figured if Tommy contacted me after reading it, it would show he was interested and willing to take the initiative.

Tommy did contact me and he was very, very excited about the concept. He initially committed to $1,500 a month, then later as I was going over things with him, he said, "You know what, I think I can do $2,000." I said, "Tommy, that's a sizable commitment. Are you *sure* you'll be able to cover your living expenses?" Especially considering he was making around $65,000 a year.

I wanted to make sure he wasn't getting in over his head. He sold me on the fact that he could stick with this. I said, "Okay," and he proved he could do that.

Just six weeks after the policy was issued, Tommy died following the motorcycle accident. And while there is no way to put a dollar value on a loved one's life, the policy did pay out a death benefit. Because the policy also included a paid-up additions rider, the value of the death benefit had already increased by almost 10 percent.

By coincidence, while I was working on this chapter, I was in a bookstore and noticed the latest book on finance by radio and talk show host Dave Ramsey. I couldn't resist seeing if he had anything new to say about whole life, and indeed he did. Using the example of someone who buys an insurance policy with a $125,000 death benefit, he states, "Worse yet, with Whole Life, the savings you finally build up after being ripped off for years don't go to your family upon your death; the only benefit paid to your family is the face value of the policy, the $125,000 of our example."

As noted earlier, Dave Ramsey, Suze Orman, and most conventional thinkers on money and finance appear to be totally unaware of the type of dividend-paying whole life policy used in Bank On Yourself, and that's a shame. Tommy's family, who saw Tommy's policy's death benefit increase by almost 10 percent in only six weeks—an increase far greater than the premiums that had been paid—wouldn't likely agree with any part of Ramsey's statement.

Following the experience with his son, Tom Snyder set up a B.O.Y. policy on his youngest child, fourteen-year-old Kelsie. It's a small policy, with a premium of $100 per month. But he wants to educate her on the value of starting early.

> I'm hoping to show her what $100 a month can do and hoping she'll do what Tommy did and open a Bank On Yourself policy of her own in a few years.

Will Medical Expenses Not Covered by Medicare Wipe You Out?

Bill Liebler, a software sales manager for one of the country's largest computer companies, might count Dick Nelson and the Gammons among the lucky ones in having a specific retirement income figure in mind. Bill says, "Of everything I've thought about, looked at, and tried to dig through, I think one of the biggest fallacies that people face is 'Oh, I'll need a lot less when I retire.' Which I definitely don't believe." He adds, "I'm assuming I'm going to need 80 percent of my working income."

Bill still may be underestimating how much he'll need to have a comfortable lifestyle in retirement. According to a 2008 survey, those in the know—folks who've already retired—found they actually required 95 percent of their preretirement income.

In fact, a lot of experts now say you should count on having 110 percent of your preretirement income (with one 2008 study by Hewitt Associates finding that, on average, people will need to replace 126 percent of their preretirement income), because you have to factor in literally hundreds of thousands of dollars it's estimated you'll need just for medical expenses not covered by Medicare. And even the very survival of Medicare is in question.

Bill:

That scares the heck out of many people these days, including me.

Bill knows there's a way he'll be able to take a retirement income from his B.O.Y. plan without owing taxes on it, under current tax law. But another thing in the tax code that works in Bill's favor—as it could for everyone else who maintains a Bank On Yourself plan—is that he'll be able to take money from his B.O.Y. policy and not have it be counted for alternative minimum tax purposes or against his Social Security earnings.

When you take retirement income from a B.O.Y. policy, it's not counted for alternative minimum tax purposes and won't lower the amount of Social Security you get.

Many people want to get their Social Security benefits as soon as they're eligible, partly because they're justifiably concerned about how much longer the fund will be able to continue paying benefits. They know that if they wait longer, they'll get a higher payment, but they need the money or want the money now. Currently, at least, taking income from your B.O.Y. plan is not going to lower the amount of Social Security earnings you get. This gives you a huge advantage.

A Former Marine Plans Ahead for Early Retirement

Advertising man Alan Twelkemeier, a six-footer with brown hair and a Tom Cruise haircut, has a fairly unusual hobby.

Alan:

> I'm an avid tournament bass fisherman. I try and get out two to
> three times a month, if time permits. If I fish a tournament, then
> I'm sure to return the favor and let my wife, Rachael, pick up on *her*
> favorite activity, which is shopping. Imagine that.

That remark may not be politically correct these days but brought a
laugh all around.

Alan believes his earlier service in the Marine Corps was a formative
experience, making him more "disciplined, not scared to tackle a project, to jump on an opportunity and know there's absolutely no way
you can't do it, if you go after it." Perhaps the Marine Corps service
also gave him a determination about his future. When we spoke, even
at the young age of thirty-two, Alan was clear about his long-term goal.

> I plan on retiring before sixty-five. That's a major consideration, and
> I know I want to have access to the funds in my retirement plan
> without restrictions.

During his years as an account executive for a media corporation,
Alan had been funding a 401(k) and then had started his first B.O.Y.
policy, a small one with a $200 a month premium. Shortly before our
conversation, he had left the security of the corporate world to become an independent contractor at another agency. That called for
some financial decisions.

> When my B.O.Y. Advisor ran the numbers and I looked at the po-
> tential tax implications, I decided I'd much rather take the early
> withdrawal penalty at this point than have to pay the potential taxes
> on my 401(k) at age sixty-five.

Instead, the advisor helped him do what's known as a pension
rollover. He took money out of his 401(k) as a pension plan distribution and used those funds as the first year's premium for his second
policy. The amount remaining in his retirement plan was then rolled
over into an annuity that would provide $3,000 a year over the next
six years to fund his newest B.O.Y. plan. Alan was confident that after
the six years, he'd be able to pay the premium out of his cash flow.

Finding enjoyment in his work, Alan doesn't expect to walk away even when he's financially in a position to do that.

It probably wouldn't be an official retirement with a gold watch and a retirement party, "See you later," and all that. I'll probably still be involved and handle some clients and still have an income.

But what made him feel so strongly about gaining control of his retirement funds that he was willing to pay the income taxes plus a 10 percent early withdrawal penalty to move his nest egg into a B.O.Y. plan? He didn't hesitate before answering.

B.O.Y. is a legitimate way to recapture my money, have it in a safe place, and not have the restrictions the government puts on retirement plans. I'm somewhat analytical, and if you use logic to look at B.O.Y., your skepticism should go out the window, because it does make sense. And it does work.

For Alan, the process of learning about B.O.Y. led him to think back over his own childhood messages about money and helped to clarify what he hopes to pass along to his children about financial matters.

My parents gave us a wonderful life. When I was growing up, there weren't many vacations or extravagant purchases, but I never felt that we were on the lower end of things. There were folks that did not have as much as we did, for sure, and of course there were always folks that had the right jeans and shoes and cars and that type of thing.
    In my home, it was more of "Can we have this?" "No, you can't. We don't have the money."
    I'd like my children to know mainly that time moves faster than you can possibly imagine, so every decision that you make needs to be considered for the future, whether it be financial or personal.

Shortly after my interview with Alan, he couldn't wait to tell me that he had just booked the first vacation he and his wife, Rachael, were taking since their honeymoon eight years ago: one week at a luxurious, all-inclusive resort on the Mexican Riviera.

All these years we couldn't justify taking a vacation because we always felt like those funds should be saved or used for something else. And we hated the idea of financing it with a loan or on a charge card, and then having to pay all that interest and have the stress of making payments for what seems like forever.

But now we don't have any guilt about it because we're financing our vacation using our Bank On Yourself plan, so we'll get the full cost of the trip back in a year, and now we'll be able to take a nice vacation *every* year from now on with those same dollars. The key words are *no guilt,* because Bank On Yourself is a responsible way to do good things for yourself that you normally wouldn't do.

"Because we're financing our vacation using our B.O.Y. plan, we'll get the full cost of the trip back in a year and be able to take a nice vacation *every* year from now on with those same dollars. There's no guilt, because it's a responsible way to do good things for yourself."

And even though Alan and Rachael had started their first B.O.Y. plan only eighteen months earlier, they'd already joined the ranks of Americans able to enjoy more of life's luxuries—without the guilt. By buying these things the Spend and Grow Wealthy Way, they *don't* have to choose between having the things they want or saving for a secure financial future.

CHAPTER 8

Eliminating Debt and Increasing Savings

For many who have become fans of Bank On Yourself, a powerful motivator has been one that you might not expect: getting out from under the burden of excessive debt.

Dancing Out of Debt and Changing People's Lives

One person finding a way out of debt through B.O.Y. is, among other things, a dancer, dance instructor, and entrepreneur of a business based around dancing.

Rose Hillbrand:

I originally came to Ohio to go to graduate school and I really ended up liking it and meeting a lot of people, and I ended up staying here. I have friends that call Ohio "the flypaper state": no one leaves once they get here.

I'm a part-time ballroom dance teacher, which is really just a hobby. And I have an Internet business as well—I sell dance shoes. I got in at the beginning; there were only a few people doing it at the time, so I'm pretty well established. I sell a lot of custom-made shoes, so people can pick all their colors and their heels and so on. That's my niche.

When I first got out of college, I dabbled in the stock market a little bit, and I was like, "Oh, this is really interesting." I had a couple hundred dollars here and there in a few different things, and I was always checking on, "Has it gone up? Has it gone down?"

Seeing everything that's been going on with the market, I'm just like, "Oh, I'm so thankful that I don't even have to think about it or pay any attention to that." Because I know that my money in my

B.O.Y. plan is safe and secure, and I'm able to use it and get to it
when I want to. It's great.

Rose, a petite redhead with a smile that lights up a room, managed
to get through college without relying heavily on student loans. However, she turned to the loan programs to get through graduate school,
where she majored in library and information science. Weighing even
more heavily on her was the credit card debt she began running up.

In graduate school, I was working, but only part time, so I wasn't really making enough to live on, and I accumulated quite a bit of debt
at that time. When I finished graduate school I was twenty-four and
I had around $30,000 total on three cards, plus about $15,000 in
student loans.
    I paid some of it off when I got a job just out of grad school, but
then I guess I figured I had plenty of time, and I didn't pay the rest
of them off. Then when I moved to Ohio I wasn't making very
much at the job that I had teaching dance full time, so I ended up
building up that debt instead of paying it down. I was driving a Ply-
mouth Horizon that was about ten years old, so I had repair expenses on top of everything else.

She was padding her income for basic living expenses by paying for
things on the credit cards that her salary couldn't cover.

I didn't feel like I was digging myself out. I felt like I was digging
myself deeper in. I felt pretty hopeless at that time. I couldn't think
of any way to get out of the hole that I was in. That's what made me
desperate to meet with somebody after I heard about B.O.Y., and
that's when I was referred to a B.O.Y. Advisor here.

The financial pit that Rose had landed in is familiar to a lot of people these days. "I just don't think people really know there's a better
way to get rid of debt," Rose says.
    About two years after starting her first B.O.Y. policy, Rose took a
policy loan.

The first thing that I used my policy for was to pay off my debt, and
I started with my smallest debt, which was the car. At that time I

owed about $2,100 on it and I went ahead and knocked that out first. I got such a feeling of satisfaction and completion by actually eliminating one debt completely. It's a great feeling.

"The first thing I used my policy for was to pay off debt, and I started with my smallest debt first. I got such a feeling of satisfaction by eliminating one debt completely."

Then a couple of months later, I paid off the student loan debt, because that was down then to just a couple thousand and I could knock that out totally as well. Oh, it was wonderful! I remember I made a list of the debts I had left, and that was only a couple of credit cards, so it was really good.

Once a person starts to pay off things that have been weighing them down for so long, the process begins to pick up momentum. Life feels as if it's going in their favor. That's the point when Bank On Yourself clients grow even more enthusiastic than they were at first. Rose recognized that description of the experience.

Oh, yes, totally! I mean, I always thought, "Wow, this is such a great idea and such a great concept." Then it started working for me and I was like, "Wow, this is really cool. I'm paying myself back, and it's really working like they said it would."

Now it's *really* working, and I'm more excited about it all the time.

I definitely feel more positive and hopeful, and not just for me, but also for people that I know that I've shared B.O.Y. with. I have a couple of friends who have started policies. And my mom is actually finally going to start something. I'm really happy about that because I know that she'll have money for her retirement.

Does Bank On Yourself change people? It did for Rose, so much so that she ended up going to work for the B.O.Y. Authorized Advisor who had guided her through the B.O.Y. process and designed her plan.

Working so closely with a B.O.Y. Advisor has broadened her understanding of B.O.Y. and gives her the opportunity to share her knowledge and enthusiasm with others.

> I feel like I am a lot more confident financially because I actually
> have a plan to get where I want to go. Before, I had no idea what to
> do. I was just like, "Oh, maybe I should invest in the market. Maybe
> I should save." I didn't know what I was doing, and I don't think
> most people do.
>
> You're not taught this in school. You're not taught much about
> anything financial in school, and I just had no idea. Now I feel like I
> know so much more than I did and than most people do. It makes
> me feel a lot more confident, hopeful, and positive—like, "Wow! I
> can change my life, and working in the office of a B.O.Y. Advisor, I
> can also help change other people's lives as well."

Rose is a great example of how even starting small can have a big
impact. The premium on her plan is $2,500 a year, and after consult-
ing with her advisor, she decided to use the funds she had in a small
IRA to pay the premium for the first couple years, until her cash flow
improved. As we wrapped up the interview, Rose commented that she
had just started her second B.O.Y. policy, with a monthly premium of
$500.

> I'm very excited! The premium isn't taking anything extra out of my
> pocket. It's just what I had been paying to reduce debt before. Now
> that it's all paid off, I can put the cash flow that was freed up into
> my new B.O.Y. plan.

* * *

A Retired Minister Gets Sucked into Low-Interest-Rate
Credit Card Offers

Retired minister Harry Peatt ("Doc Hank," as he prefers to be called)
was a man who supplemented his modest church income by holding

other jobs at the same time, managing to live well enough and maintain a perfect credit record.

Doc Hank:

> I've never been in the situation in my life of not making my monthly payment to a credit card. But then a bank, because of my wonderful credit, would offer me $10,000, $15,000, $20,000, or something for one year at zero percent, and I would take it. At the end of the year, I would have to find another zero percent offer. So that became my style.

Bank On Yourself to the rescue. Not long after he started his first policy, he was in position to take a loan.

> I had $30,000 out in credit card debt and a home equity line of credit. I took a first B.O.Y. loan out, and with it I paid off all the debt.

Chalk up one more person who used B.O.Y. as a rescue ladder from credit card and other debt. And now he's profiting from the interest that had been making others rich.

More about Doc Hank later on.

A Surgeon Climbs Out from Under Crushing Medical School Debt

Dr. Jerry West is a thirty-six-year-old surgeon. Over six feet tall, with a lean build, brown hair, and blue eyes, he could play the role of a surgeon on television. His office looks out over a resort town in the Southwest, known for its challenging golf courses.

> My father was a stockbroker who worked for one of the major brokerage houses for twenty years. We were always told to save. We were taught to try to be smart with our money or frugal or cheap, however you want to describe it. We didn't waste money on many things.
>
> My dad did a financial seminar he had recorded and I was just watching the DVD this past week. He spoke favorably of insurance even at that time and he himself purchased a fair amount. He saw the need and the role of insurance. He was definitely not a radical in

the sense of thinking stocks were the only way to go. He had a realistic view of the market and the dangers. He had seen people make tons of money but he had also seen people lose their shirts, too.

He started me and my brother out on investing in mutual funds when we were just eight or nine. He was fairly conservative in the way he invested and encouraged that. That was the money I had on hand when I got married. That's what I used to buy my wedding ring. It exhausted the account.

Jerry's wife grew up with messages that were "somewhat similar," he says.

But we definitely have different ways of looking at money. I wouldn't say she's a spender, but she's more of a spender than I am. It's funny —when we first got married, that was a little bit of a shock. I think most couples have that. I think I've loosened up a little bit, and she's tightened up a little bit as time's gone on.

Becoming a surgeon, or for that matter a medical specialist of any sort, means four years of college, four years of medical school, and then earning a small income as an intern and a resident for another several years. Before the new doctor can earn any sort of income to live on, he or she has put in perhaps thirteen years, most of that time shelling out for tuition, books, housing, food, and all the other usual living expenses.

So how much debt had Jerry run up by the time he was ready to go into practice?

I had some family loans and some government loans. In total it was about $280,000 of student debt. All of the earlier loans continued accruing interest during the five years of internship and residency. It just eats away at you.

Through all those years, we're all thinking, "Well, we're going to be doctors. We're going to make a good income, and it just comes with the territory."

That's a big problem. You think of physicians as being smart, but financially there are a lot of terrible choices that people make of getting loans they don't need, because they think, "No big deal, I'll pay it back."

A cardiologist who was training at the same place as me was one of those smart people that really just don't know how to deal with money. It's one of those things where you wonder, "What is he thinking?" He got into a home based on what he was "going" to make. I mean, it was just insane, and the amount of credit card debt this guy had, you just scratch your head. You can *always* spend more than you make. And he wasn't the only one.

He and his wife gave up their house and they moved to a whole different area. It was bad. I mean, he was making hundreds of thousands of dollars and still not able to pay his bills. It just blows you away.

But even for someone handling his student expenses a great deal more sensibly, it still wasn't easy for Jerry.

I borrowed from family as much as possible because I knew they'd be nice to me on the interest rate. But I definitely had anxiety on the amount of debt I was getting into.

On the loans I took from my mother, the way I'm paying her back is with one of my Bank On Yourself policies. It's set up to pay her off over a twenty-year period. The way we set it up was that I'm paying this insurance policy for her that will go to her beneficiaries when she dies. My concern was about being fair to my three brothers, who want that estate filled back up when she dies.

But Jerry's first policy—he had just started his sixth and seventh when we spoke—went to a different purpose. His advisor showed him how much he would gain by taking out a B.O.Y. plan and borrowing against it to pay off his car loan.

He showed me how I would be losing hundreds of thousands of dollars over the years on my car purchases if I paid for them the usual way, with loans or by leasing. That got to me pretty quickly. So my initial policy I started with a $10,000 annual premium and fairly soon after took a loan of about $8,000. I used that to pay off the outstanding loan on my Suburban and then started making those monthly car payments to my B.O.Y. plan instead.

It didn't take Jerry very long to start getting back the cost of his car purchases. He can now recycle those dollars over and over again for the rest of his life to finance his own cars. By doing so, he'll recapture hundreds of thousands of dollars that would have gone out the window and be able to use that money however he wants. And that's the impact of doing this for just *one* of his family's cars.

A policy loan can also be used in another powerful way that I call leveraging.

I'm looking into using a loan from one of my policies to purchase shares in a surgical center. This is a medical building with four operating rooms and all the related equipment and facilities where I do much of my surgery.

After this interview, Jerry did go ahead with taking a policy loan to buy shares in the center. How is this an example of leverage?

Recall that money borrowed from a Bank On Yourself policy continues to earn the same annual cash value increases, as well as the same dividends. Jerry has used the money he borrowed from his policy toward the shares he purchased in the surgical center, which provide an excellent return on his investment. So his money is doing double duty for him: growing in his B.O.Y. plans as though he had never touched a dime of it, and at the same time invested in a way that is earning him a profit. That's the art of leverage: having the same funds at work for you in two different ways simultaneously.

Jerry leveraged the equity in his B.O.Y. plan when he borrowed from it to purchase shares in a surgical center. Leveraging allows you to have the same funds at work for you in two different ways simultaneously.

Jerry described how it feels to cash in on this remarkable feature of Bank On Yourself.

It's almost like you feel like you've been getting ripped off and now you're not going to get ripped off anymore. Knowing that your money truly is doing double duty for you, it's just the best of both worlds.

Jerry has gotten some flack from his CPA, who has the standard Suze Orman/Dave Ramsey party line on insurance. Jerry's comment:

The majority of Americans invest in the traditional way, and most people are *not* doing well, so there's got to be something else, something better. I have friends and it's interesting to hear them talk about investing, what they're in and how it's been a bad day or bad week, or whatever.

I can see why some people may get a little impatient with Bank On Yourself. In the early years of a policy, it does take awhile to build up value. But once it gets going and you're using your own money, that's where the excitement is—for me, anyway. And knowing what my kids will be able to do with B.O.Y.

Asked what advice he would give to readers of this book, Jerry replied:

It would be, "Don't discount this idea." It's a long-term solution to take control of all your finances. You need to be patient with it in the beginning, but it's a terrific long-term strategy.

CHAPTER 9

Never Too Rich or Too Cash-Strapped to Bank On Yourself

Perhaps one of the most fascinating aspects of Bank On Yourself is that some wealthy people who hear about it tend to think it makes sense only for 9-to-5 working folks, or people laden with heavy credit-card debt. Meanwhile, people who worry about whether there will be enough cash to last through to the end of the month or who are saddled with a burden of debt think there's no way they could afford it.

Both those assumptions are usually wrong, as the examples in this chapter show.

B.O.Y. Turns a Spender into a Saver—Without Giving Up Life's Luxuries

Along with his wife, Gene Pittman, a Texas software engineer, is one among the legion of American families who march to the tune of the consumer economy.

Gene:

My wife, Sheryl, and I were using our income to live and to pay off debt, and then everything we had left over we were just spending, just wasting.

Sheryl was putting just enough into her 401(k) to meet the match, and that was it. I'm one of those live-one-day-at-a-time kind of people. No savings, not really thinking of the future, just having fun.

I would go through stages where I would think about it, but then I would put it aside. I got to the point where I thought, "Okay. I'm in my forties now. I need to make some changes. It's time." But I was not disciplined enough to do anything.

Gene's way of taking vacations before he discovered Bank On Yourself reveals an experience similar to the one described by Alan Twelke-meier (chapter 7) and that many readers can probably relate to.

I wanted to really romance my wife. I went out and planned a vacation over to San Diego for just the two of us to get away. But once we got over there, she was miserable.

I didn't realize what I had done. I got us to San Diego, but then I was putting the squash on going to do anything, because we didn't really have the money to go do all the extra stuff. She was really frustrated.

I realized that's exactly what I had been doing all along. I'd start feeling guilty and then I'd try to figure out how I was going to fix it.

One evening after his Bible study group, Gene shared his frustrations with another member of the group.

I knew this man was in the financial industry, and I knew that he was very, very successful. So it just opened up a door for me to be honest with him about my frustrations about how easy it has always been for me to go down and take out a loan at the bank.

He said, "Let me share with you this concept that I've been introduced to." He was a B.O.Y. Advisor. He was an answer to a prayer.

Now, by buying things using my B.O.Y. plan, it takes the guilt away because that's *my* money, and I'm paying it right back to myself. It takes away all of that frustration. It actually frees you up to be able to enjoy life.

> "By buying things using a B.O.Y. plan, it takes all the guilt away and frees you up to enjoy life."

We started out initially with two policies, one for my wife and one for me. Together, the premium is $1,220 a month.

Gene credits his banking-related experience to the fact that B.O.Y. struck a chord right away for him:

I test software that's used by major banks, auto- and mortgage-lending companies. After twenty-five years, I've really been able to grasp how the banking industry works as a result of working with the software. So the B.O.Y. concept immediately made sense to me. Where it became very interesting was how a B.O.Y.-designed life insurance policy complemented it, because I didn't understand how these policies worked.

Now I look at my whole financial picture from the perspective a banker would take. If I were to own the bank on the corner here, I'd want everybody's money to flow through my bank, because that means I'm going to be making more money. So for the same reason, I want as much of my own money and cash flow funneling through my Bank On Yourself plans as I possibly can. I just keep thinking how brilliant it is that somebody came up with this idea.

Gene couldn't wait to start using the money growing in his B.O.Y. plans to become his own financing source.

My wife just felt like we had to have a pool, because my son needed a pool. Happy wife, happy life. So we took out our first policy loan to go buy a $3,500 above-ground pool.

I wanted to start paying it back immediately. I looked at my finances, and I called my B.O.Y. Advisor. He said, "How much interest do you want to pay?"

I said, "I think I'm worth 10 percent." So that's what I did.

When Gene talks about being "worth 10 percent," he's referring to the Spend and Grow Even Wealthier method of paying a little extra every month over the interest rate the insurance company charges on policy loans. Gene's advisor had designed his plan so that extra amount would go into his paid-up additions rider, where it will work its turbo-charging magic.

Picking an interest rate, like 10 percent, for example, makes it simple to run a loan amortization schedule to calculate what you want your monthly loan payment to be. Gene discussed why he found it easy to be disciplined in paying back the loan he took from his B.O.Y. plan.

I think a lot of people think, "Okay, I'm just going to sit on my B.O.Y. plan. I don't want to take any money from my policy." You're not doing yourself any favors by doing that, because of the way these policies work.

To me, I was just paying back a commitment that I had already been disciplined to make to other people's banks and finance companies. But what was really cool is when I stopped to realize that "Hey, that 'bank' is me!" It was almost like this is too good to be true, but it was awesome.

In fact, many people who have started Bank On Yourself refer to their plan the way Gene does, as if it were the bank on the corner. They'll say, "I took a loan from my bank," meaning from their B.O.Y. plan. It's a handy term, but I sometimes worry that it can be misleading. Of course, a B.O.Y. plan is a life insurance policy, not an actual bank or savings and loan company.

Still, I understand why people talk about their plan like that: it can work like the bank on the corner in some ways, ready to lend you money for any good purpose, a loan that you then pay back each month. So I always make sure people understand this when they refer to their plan as "my bank." Otherwise my watchdog attorneys might get stuffy about it.

Gene described the unexpected benefits he and his wife received by financing their pool through their B.O.Y. plans, in addition to recapturing the purchase price and interest they would have paid if they had instead taken out an installment loan.

We were really excited, because now we had a place that not only my son but *all* the kids in the neighborhood could come to. We felt like our home became a safe environment that would allow us to keep an eye on where our son was, who was with him, and to be able to enjoy more of his childhood with him and create great memories for all of us.

My number-one priority is to get myself out of destructive debt and then start living life the way I want to live it. I always used to think, "What can we afford to do on vacation? Well, I guess we can go to another city here in Texas." Now I'm thinking, "Well, shoot, let's go to Hawaii, stay at a five-star hotel, and let's experience life, create some memories, and leave the guilt behind." We never could have dreamed of that before, but if we funnel the money we'd pay for that through our B.O.Y. plans, then next year we'll be able to do it again.

It reminds me of that commercial. You can pay "X" dollars for a car, or "X" dollars for a vacation, but the memories you create are priceless, and that's what B.O.Y. is allowing me to do. It's really freed up my spirit to think, "Heck, yeah! That's doable!" It's really giving my wife and me the freedom to share dreams together.

How much of a role does Gene's B.O.Y. Advisor play in keeping him on track?

The support and advice he gives me is absolutely critical. You need to build a team and surround yourself with people who can really help you. My B.O.Y. Advisor educates me, helps me see things from different directions, and helps me make smart decisions that will help us achieve our goals. He's my partner.

> "The support and advice my Bank On Yourself Authorized Advisor gives me is absolutely critical. He helps me make smart decisions that will help us reach our goals."

Gene was so enthusiastic about how his life had already changed since he discovered B.O.Y., how it had turned him from a spender into a saver, without having to give up the things he loves, that he even started thinking of getting a supplemental job "to bring in more income to expedite the B.O.Y. process."

To put a B.O.Y. Advisor on your team who can help you make smart decisions about your money, and for a free Bank On Yourself Analysis, visit **www.BankOnYourselfFreeAnalysis.com**.

When the Market Turns Against You

We spoke with Melissa O'Brien on a day in early spring when the weather in her Connecticut hometown was windy and chilly. With a bachelor's degree in computer science, Melissa gave up her job as a computer programmer to become a stay-at-home mom. She and her husband, Tom, a salesman, had two children, a nine-year-old girl and a six-year-old boy, at the time of this conversation.

We began by talking about the financial messages she learned as a child.

Melissa:

I knew nothing about what went on financially in the house. Zero. It wasn't until much later that I found out how difficult my parents had it when I was growing up. It was very hard for them. They came from a Depression-era background.

My mother's parents owned a store and worked seven days a week. They really struggled for every penny they earned. My father's father was a farmer, and farmers struggle in their own way.

I particularly remember a story my parents told me about when they got married and they bought their first house back in 1956. They put down all their money as the required down payment, and they had exactly $20 left in their account. And that was it.

Even so, my two other siblings and I all went to private high schools. I never knew how much it was until recently. It was about $6,000 a year then for the high school. Today the private high schools run $25,000 a year. But they put the priorities where they needed to be.

I never once felt like we were deprived. It never crossed my mind. I had my ten toys growing up, and I thought that was just fine. I didn't need more than ten toys.

Talk about opposites attracting: my husband Tom's side of the family is 100 percent different. He comes from a very wealthy family, living on Park Avenue in Manhattan. His grandfather, believe it or not, was one of the founders of a well-known Wall Street firm, and Tom's mother came from the diamond business.

[Before we were married,] Tom was laid off. He found two entry-level jobs but it wasn't enough. He fell three months behind on his house payments. When he asked his parents for help, they didn't give it to him. He was shocked. It was ultimately *my* mother who ended up giving him a loan for $15,000. So he has struggled financially during his adult life, even though he comes from a very wealthy background.

Though they still have some years to go until retirement—she's forty-two, he's fifty-one—it's on their minds. A stress factor, and a motivator for finding a better solution, was their dismal experience in the stock market.

Studies show that the typical investor—and even most professional money managers—don't come anywhere close to achieving the long-term results of the overall stock market. (I referenced the sources of these studies earlier in this book.) Other studies and surveys reveal that people often overstate their investment results, either to save face or because they don't actually know what their return is. The O'Briens, however, do know.

Honestly, we did horribly in the stock market and mutual funds during the entire bull market run. We bought at the right time, but I would want to sell, and my husband didn't want to. Usually he won out, and unfortunately we lost as a result of that.

So 2001 came and blew out everything. Just to give you an idea of how poorly we did, since 1996 we've been keeping meticulous records of how we do. Since then and up through the end of last year [2007], we were up a *total* of 2.52 percent. Not 2.52 percent a year, but 2.52 percent total over eleven years that included the bull market. It's terrible!

Thank God we saved through all those times. We wouldn't be up at all if we hadn't kept putting money in. In fact, we would be down nearly 50 percent.

My husband was in the hospital just before the big tumble in 2007. Even our Bank On Yourself Advisor predicted it. He said, "Take your money out of the market. It's going to dive. The mortgage crisis is happening. Take it out, take it out, take it out."

So I go into the hospital and I tell my husband, "You know what, we've got to sell two mutual funds, take our profits, and go."

He says, "No, no, no, no." We were up, like, 80 percent in a China fund. We were just doing phenomenally well.

Then suddenly we're down to 70 percent and then 60 percent. He said, "It's going to go back up." I said, "Let's take the money and run." Now we're down to only a 10 percent gain, and we haven't sold it yet.

The greed factor gets in there. I've learned over the years to reduce that factor. He's not there yet. I love him so much, but everyone has their issues. What can I say? I told him, "You know what, you've just got to let me take over the finances."

He was finally realizing that we better do something else to get our retirement income up.

In conversations with the B.O.Y. Advisor she was referred to, she mentioned that retirement income was her husband's hot button. The advisor suggested she talk to him about how the dividends can increase over time, which brings the possibility of an increasing retirement income that wouldn't bounce around like the stock or real estate markets do.

Apparently it was a successful approach, because after three months of researching, asking questions, and running it by Melissa's sister, who had majored in insurance and confirmed that B.O.Y. was for real, they signed up for their first plans. "One for me, one for Tom, and one for each of our two kids, for a total annual premium of $60,000," according to Melissa.

We decided to pay all the premiums annually, instead of monthly. This forced Tom to agree we should sell. We had to sell mutual funds worth $60,000 to pay the first year's premium. Our advisor suggested that we sell a particular fund, which had done very, very well for a change, and we sold it at the right time. We actually made a profit on it.

I was so happy to sell that mutual fund at a profit!

The sale took care of the first year's premium. Where was the $60,000 going to come from in subsequent years?

That's approximately what we had been saving on an annual basis, which normally would have gone into another mutual fund or a 401(k). We dropped way down from the $20,000 a year we were putting in Tom's 401(k). That certainly helped. We stopped all but the $1,200 Tom's employer matches.

"We were able to start our first four B.O.Y. plans, totaling $60,000 of annual premium, by selling some of our mutual funds and dropping Tom's 401(k) contribution way down to the level his employer matches."

We have a few IRAs and 401(k)s. That's what we did because that's all we knew back then.

With so many struggling to save even a small percentage of their income, how do the O'Briens manage to put aside such a significant sum?

We're a little unusual. We actually put pressure on ourselves much more than the average person to save for retirement. We've always treated saving for retirement as an expense, a bill we have to pay.

If we're not meeting our retirement savings commitment, it puts the same stress on us that it would if we couldn't meet our mortgage payments. Or as if we were being foreclosed on the house.

What have Melissa and Tom used their plans for?

I needed a new car and took out a $25,000 loan for it. I bought a Toyota minivan, so we didn't have to lease it like I had done with my previous car. Once you use B.O.Y. to finance things yourself, you can't deny that it works.

Melissa and Tom had another big financial goal they wanted to use their B.O.Y. plans for, in addition to financing their own cars and growing a nest egg: paying off the balance on their mortgage.

I just got the checks three days ago for a total of $60,000, and we're sending the money in to pay off our mortgage in full.

Our motivation for paying off the mortgage is to know that under no circumstances will we be foreclosed upon. Tom could lose his job tomorrow and not get a new one for a year, and we know that we would have our house.

It feels fantastic to know that it's paid off. We love telling people we did so with a B.O.Y. loan. Of course, we get those looks of complete non-understanding!

When I spoke with Melissa, she and Tom had already started their tenth B.O.Y. plan and were putting a total of $120,000 a year into them.

During the interview, Melissa mentioned that her B.O.Y. plans had been structured by her B.O.Y. Advisor so that after paying the premiums from their savings and cash flow for approximately seven years, the dividends that had been credited to their plans could potentially be used to pay future premiums.

With a B.O.Y. policy, at some point, dividends being credited to the plan may potentially be used to pay future premiums.

That's another advantage of this kind of policy. Here's how it works: in many cases the plan can be designed so that when the policy owner has funded the plan for some period of time, the accumulated dividends and future dividends could be sufficient to pay future premiums. The point at which this happens depends on how much the dividends are along the way. But it can happen *much* sooner in a B.O.Y. policy than it would in a traditional whole life policy.

But Melissa and Tom don't plan to retire at that point, so they will have a couple of options: they could open a new policy and redirect the premiums into it that they had been paying out of pocket for the older plans, or they could continue funding the older plans out of their cash flow. When they reach that point, their B.O.Y. Advisor will review their options with them.

Melissa and Tom started two more plans shortly after our interview (they now have twelve), because they understand that the more plans they have, and the bigger the plans are, the more things they can finance themselves, and the more money they could have for their retirement. One thing they *won't* be missing is the nail-biting and uncertainty of the traditional investing and saving strategies they had been using.

* * *

B.O.Y. as a Turbo Charger for Wealth

A mid-thirties administrative assistant and meeting planner for a major pharmaceutical company, Lisa Sabo lives with her husband, John, and their three-year-old son in a bi-level on a quiet cul-de-sac about forty-five miles outside New York City.

Lisa:

> I volunteer for community service activities—things like going to nursing homes and doing things with the elderly there. My father-in-law used to live in one for a while before he passed away, as did my grandfather, and I think it just made me really see the need to do something nice for somebody in that situation. Being a regular visitor there, you realize that not a lot of people go to see their loved ones. It just made me really sad, so I wanted to give a little bit back because everybody was very nice to both of my relatives.

Lisa found the money for her first Bank On Yourself policy from some of the same sources as others in these pages.

> February 2004 is when I started the Bank On Yourself policy. I had another policy that, after careful consideration, I cashed in to start funding this one with. The other one had no paid-up additions rider on it, and it was growing very slowly.

Always a saver, Lisa had no problem finding money on an ongoing basis for B.O.Y. She and her husband shifted monies that were going into equities, such as mutual funds, into their first two policies.

The couple had also been contributing to a basic "safe" money market account at a very low interest rate that was their emergency fund.

We learned that B.O.Y. can serve the role of an emergency fund, as opposed to having money just sit in something that's taxable and making practically nothing.

So after the first year, the money to fund Lisa's policy and her husband's came through a shifting of savings from mutual funds, and a shifting of emergency savings funds from a bank account to their B.O.Y. policies.

A B.O.Y. policy can be flexible in other ways, as well.

We had a couple of lifestyle changes last year. I went from working full time to working part time, because I wanted to be with our son more.

I then turned to our B.O.Y. Advisor for a check-in to review our entire plan. We moved more funds to pay back the loans sooner, because there was going to be a cash-flow shortfall. We basically paid back the loans in five or six months.

Like many others, Lisa used her plan for a car purchase, a previously owned Acura with low miles, which is now paid off—so she has the car, has now recovered into the plan all the money she paid for the car, and on top of that has the interest she would have given to a finance company. How does that feel? She answered:

> "It's thrilling to see what B.O.Y. is all about when you finance something through the plan from start to finish. Once you do it, you're like, 'Wow, this is really easy and there are so many benefits.'"

It was thrilling! I got to see what it's all about from start to finish. You know you're doing good. I'm not paying interest to somebody who loaned me money. I'm, in essence, just paying myself and growing my money more. It's like fattening up the pot. Once you do it, you're like, "Wow, this is a really easy thing and there are so many great benefits."

How a Fourteen-Year-Old Girl Found the Money to B.O.Y.

Anyone concerned that they "can't afford" to start a B.O.Y. plan need look no further than the teenage children of airline captain Kevin Rowan and his wife, Susan, a teacher and horse breeder. When the Rowans decided to start their youngsters on B.O.Y. plans, they arranged the process differently than most people.

Kevin:

> I think it's great that some parents help or even fund B.O.Y. plans for their children. But there's a real value in teaching them how to do something for themselves. I think one of the biggest problems is that we don't teach our kids anything about money or finances in school. I mean, my daughter got out of high school without even knowing how to balance a checkbook, for crying out loud.

The Rowans introduced their two daughters to their B.O.Y. Advisor when Andrea was eighteen and Kaitlin was just fourteen. Andrea, who was going to school to become a dental assistant and also worked, decided to start her own plan with a $134 a month premium. The monthly payment was comparable to what her car payment was, and financing her own car was Andrea's first goal for her plan.

Kaitlin funded her B.O.Y. plan with a $50 monthly premium. And where did the fourteen-year-old find the money to pay for it? According to her mother, "Kaitlin works part time cleaning up manure for our horse stable, and other chores."

I thought that was a perfect example of the saying "Where there's a will, there's a way." And what better way to teach your children about money than to show them how to turn the direction of the flow of money in their lives *to* them, instead of away from them, at an early age?

You'll find more from the Rowans in chapter 11.

* * *

In the preceding stories, we've looked at the situations of people whose financial picture ranges from modest to comfortable. To wrap up, we look at a family in the position to afford the very best financial advice money can buy, and who have made the same choice as the others in accepting the wisdom of Bank On Yourself.

A Dentist Turns Financial Decision-Maker

Dr. David Knightley is a man in an enviable position. As an endodontist, or root-canal dentist, he enjoys a seven-figure income and a net worth of several million dollars. The dentist and his wife, Emma, live on the West Coast with their four teenage children. A lot of people with money like that would be living lavishly. He and Emma don't live by those values.

David:

> We're not big spenders. We live in a house in the suburbs that we bought eighteen years ago. We do take a vacation generally in the spring and then try to do something in the summer. Those probably are the largest single expenses other than the living expenses.

An earlier experience with life insurance might have been enough to sour him about considering Bank On Yourself, at least for someone less open-minded than David.

> When I was a graduate student, about twenty years ago, I bought a whole life policy.

Even a whole life policy that does not have all the features of the kind used for Bank On Yourself should have grown a nice-sized cash value over a twenty-year period. David's didn't.

> I was convinced to get rid of it by the firm that does money management for me. They said that term life is best. They said, "You shouldn't be using whole life because you can get the same amount of insurance coverage for a lot less money, and you can invest the

difference in the cost of the premium in an asset-allocated plan that will stay so many percentage points above inflation."

In spite of that, when the doctor heard about Bank On Yourself, it made sense to him.

I'm always trying to think a little bit differently and be open to alternative ideas for saving and investing, and this one caught my attention.

I thought that this might be an excellent way to not rely so much on the usual retirement type of planning that goes on that I was already involved with. Also, it appeared that there are some aspects that may be good for my children and that maybe can even transcend one generation and beyond.

The idea of having funds available for estate taxes when one dies and being able to pass wealth on to the next generation—I had a little familiarity with that, so that was also an aspect of this that intrigued me.

Another of the doctor's points provides an additional example of the leverage discussed earlier.

One of the best ways to use B.O.Y., I think, is to fund the plan and then invest the cash values. If you invested it in mutual funds, for example, you'd come out ahead, because you continue to get growth on the money you borrowed from your plan.

David started with two policies for himself, two for his wife, and one policy for each of their four children, a total of eight policies. Shortly before we spoke, he had started two additional plans. His total annual premium for the ten plans was $240,000.

And what does David's money manager think about his decision to put such a sizable sum into his B.O.Y. plans?

To be honest, I haven't even told my other financial advisors about this. More than 99 percent either aren't aware of this or don't understand it. I don't want the abuse. At some point you're old enough to make your own decisions. I weighed the evidence and decided this is what I really want to do.

> "I haven't even told my other financial
> advisors about this. More than 99 percent
> either aren't aware of this or don't
> understand it. At some point you're old
> enough to make your own decisions."

David plans to use his B.O.Y. policies to help fund his retirement, invest in real estate, and aid in putting his four children through college—which is fast approaching for all of them.

And, like others in these pages, he has turned his thoughts to educating his children on the virtues of Bank On Yourself.

I'm fifty-four now. I realized the advantage this has for the next generation, and that's what I was thinking in terms of giving the kids a real head start on their policies. Starting at a young age, even with a small amount, this is just an unbelievable way to accumulate wealth.

CHAPTER 10

The Spend and Grow Wealthy Way to Pay for College

An e-mail I received from a subscriber to my Bank On Yourself Success Tips newsletter broke my heart. It read in part, "I work three jobs . . . my day job that starts at 7 a.m. and ends at 3 or 4 p.m. . . . a lawn-care business in the afternoon, and I deliver papers from 2 a.m. to 5:30 a.m.—all to pay for college for my daughter. How do I get a referral to a Bank On Yourself Authorized Advisor?"

Finding the money for a college education can be a daunting prospect. For too many families, it means paying for college with money that *could* have gone to finance their retirement and to enjoy more of life's luxuries.

And using student loans saddles the graduate with debt that averages $20,000. Ten percent of undergraduates leave college with debt of $35,000 or more. That's a tough way to start out in life.

Can B.O.Y. really let you recapture the cost of a college education? The people we interviewed gave us a universally enthusiastic yes.

An Excusable Late-in-Life Start to College Funding

A cabin in the woods makes a nearly ideal setting for a conversation on topics that range from the general to the highly personal. This particular cabin is a small, rustic cottage with pine wood paneling and a stone fireplace, in the Blue Ridge Mountains of North Carolina, at an elevation of 4,800 feet. The setting offers a view to a distance of about one hundred miles, across thousands of acres of preserved forest as well as three ski slopes.

This tranquil, rugged property is owned by a man quoted earlier in these pages, software sales manager Bill Liebler, along with his wife, Meloney, and two of the Lieblers' friends. When I spoke with Bill by phone, he described their acre of land as offering "nothing but hardwood trees and rocks with tons of deer and wild turkey and other critters running around." Does that suggest Bill might be a hunter? Quite the opposite.

I'm married to a tree-hugger, so if I showed up with a dead animal, I'd be the next one shot. It's a place for trout fishing, golfing, and mountain hiking. And for just getting away. We love the mountains.

For most people, forty-seven years old would seem to be late in life to begin thinking about funding a child's college education. But not for Bill Liebler. Seventeen years into their marriage, the couple received a happy surprise.

We just assumed all those years that we couldn't have children. My father-in-law was a Baptist minister. After he retired, he was diagnosed with cancer. He passed away thirty days later, and about six months after that, my wife was pregnant.
     I just figured he needed to do some "networking."
     Not long ago I wrote an article for a friend of mine's Web site called "First-Time Fatherhood at a Medically Advanced Age." So I do have a sense of humor about it, but I also realize I'm going to be sixty when my daughter starts college. When she finishes undergrad school, we'll be sixty-four or sixty-five.

(Note to everyone thinking of giving up on starting a family late in life: Bill says having Shelby in their lives is "just a lot of fun.")
     The most common methods used by families saving for college for their youngsters include traditional investment and savings accounts, UGMAs (Uniform Gift to Minors Accounts), and 529 college savings plans (so called after the section of the Internal Revenue Code that sets out the rules for this type of college savings; they are also known as qualified tuition plans). Not knowing at the time that there was a better way, the Lieblers started funding a 529 plan for Shelby's college. That changed after Bill learned about B.O.Y. and was referred to a B.O.Y. Advisor.

When my advisor and I first sat down to talk about this, I told him my plan was to fund the 529 plan for the first few years as aggressively as I could. Things were going pretty well income-wise, so I figured, "Fund it while you've got some extra cash flow."

I had planned all along to fund it for four or five years at a certain rate, and put money from Grandma into it, too. My advisor said, "I'm not a big fan of these 529 plans because of the restrictions. They're not very flexible." He's right.

Let's say your child gets a scholarship. If you've got a 529 plan, you don't need it anymore because of your child's scholarship, but there are restrictions against using the money for anything but education. Or if Shelby doesn't go to college, with her being an only child, my wife and I would have to go take some college classes with the money in a 529 plan, or wait until we're fifty-nine and a half to avoid paying penalties.

Otherwise we'll have to pay taxes on the gains as well as penalties to use that money.

Bill's advisor expanded on the explanation.
Advisor:

The beautiful thing about using Bank On Yourself as the alternative is that if the child doesn't go to school or gets a scholarship, then you've got additional money you can use for your retirement, or however and whenever you want, for that matter. And the money can do double duty by your taking out a policy loan and using it to remodel your kitchen or whatever, as opposed to a 529 plan, which cannot be used that way.

Using a Bank On Yourself plan to finance
a college education gives you flexibility
and many advantages you don't get with
a 529 plan, UGMA, investment, or
savings account.

With a B.O.Y. plan, you don't have the risk of loss due to market fluctuations. What if you're saving in a 529 plan, and the market tanks shortly before your child is ready to go to college? *Now* what are you going to do?

Bill chimed in:

That's a great point. Shelby's 529 plan is down this year. Not only is
it inflexible when it comes to how you can use the money, but also
how you can invest the money. I can't easily pick up the phone and
call a broker and say, "The market's tanking. Get out of those mutual funds and put it in cash or bonds." You have to move it between funds. With B.O.Y., I never even have to worry about that
happening.

Bill discovered still another advantage.

If you want to apply for college financial aid for your child, the
money in the B.O.Y. policy does not count against you for financial aid.

In saying this, Bill means that when you list your assets on the
Free Application for Federal Student Aid (FAFSA), you could have
$100,000 cash value in your B.O.Y. policy, or several hundred thou-
sand, but it would not count against you for the purposes of judging
whether you qualify for college financial aid or scholarships. The
same amount of assets in regular savings accounts, UGMA accounts,
stock market accounts, or real estate could make your youngster
ineligible.

Also, as mentioned earlier, when you take retirement income from
a B.O.Y. plan, it's not counted toward your earnings limit for Social
Security—it won't cause you to lose Social Security benefits.

As you can guess, once Bill discovered all the strings and restrictions that came with his 529 plan, he stopped funding it and started
funding a B.O.Y. plan instead. Now he's in the unique situation of
having friends and coworkers his own age with kids ready to start college who didn't know about B.O.Y. and used conventional college
funding methods.

The last thing that we would want to be staring at now, like a number of my friends are who are my age with kids going into college, is
they are coming out of college and not only are the children holding
a big loan, but the parents have either refinanced their house or

they've taken out a home equity credit line or they've taken out college loans. They're starting to pay off those loans over a period of time and that's taking away from their lifestyle and their retirement.

"A lot of my friends who didn't know about B.O.Y. are now paying off loans they took for their kids' college education and it's taking away from their lifestyle and their retirement. That's the last thing we'd want to be staring at now."

It can be pretty daunting. One of my friends has done this in a very logical way. He and his wife have six kids. Three of them are out of college, one just finished, and the other two are finishing up. He and I have had some pretty long talks about that, and how they've been able to juggle things versus what the kids have taken on.

He and his wife have struggled, refinancing the house and pulling out some money and also feeling uncomfortable that all six of his children are coming out of college with at least some degree of student loan debt and knowing that they've got to start their working life that way. It was a constant juggle of cash flow and making decisions about what they could and couldn't do. It really produced a limiting factor on their lifestyle and budget. Not that they would trade it for their kids in any way, but that's just the financial reality of the story.

They had them go to state schools. They've done a lot of things, but you look at six kids times, who knows, $60,000? They've probably spent between $250,000 and $300,000 to send them to school.

I had student loans coming out of college, so I don't think that's a terrible route to go, but at the same time you look at that and know it's not a good way to start off your working and financial life. That clearly was a big factor in working with my advisor on deciding to use B.O.Y. to fund Shelby's college.

Bill then explained how he was making his B.O.Y. plan work even harder by using the equity in his plan to finance other things the Spend and Grow Even Wealthier way, while building the money to pay for Shelby's college.

I just borrowed $40,000 from my B.O.Y. plan; $26,000 of that we
used to pay for the new car we just bought for my wife. We're "drive
cars until they die" people and hers was eight years old. It's pretty
cool. It's like writing ourselves a check every month. It's not just that
we're paying ourselves back, it's also an investment into our future.

It's also knowing that if something goes bump in the night, or
cash flow is tight for a month or two or three, I could delay making
some payments and not have somebody breathing down my neck.

And what did Bill do with the remaining $14,000 he borrowed
from his plan?

As part of buying our vacation cabin, my two partners and I are having the basement finished and putting a deck on and a hot tub in. I
used the other $14,000 I borrowed to pay for my part of finishing
the basement, so now I'll be paying myself back.

The conversation then turned to the market conditions at the time
of the interview, in spring 2008. Referring to the value of his stocks,
Bill said, "It goes down by the day." The comment led me to share a
story about what had recently happened in my own household. One
evening after dinner, I heard my husband, Larry, yelling from the den,
"You've got to get over here, quick. I just can't believe this. You've *got*
to see this!" He was pointing at his computer screen looking like he'd
seen a ghost. He had discovered that our pension plan had lost over
$6,700 in just that one day.

We had this deal that neither of us was going to look at our plan
balances more than once every few months, and we'd checked it out a
few weeks before, so I'm standing there going, "What are you doing
looking at that? Why are you torturing yourself?" The plan had lost
25 percent over the previous year and a half, the value of our home
was down 22 percent, and Larry was saying, "We can't afford these
kinds of losses now—we've only got ten years left until retirement."

I had to grab the file I keep of annual statements from all eighteen
of our B.O.Y. plans and show him how much each one had increased
over the past year, between the guaranteed cash value increase and the
dividends. One plan had gone up the previous year by more than two
and a half times our annual premium (which stays constant through-

out the life of the policy). And nine years from now, when I turn
sixty-four, that plan is projected to increase by around five times the
annual premium.

> "Every one of our family's eighteen B.O.Y.
> plans increased more this year (as the stock
> and real estate markets were tanking) than
> they did last year. One plan went up by
> more than two and a half times our annual
> premium, and nine years from now, when I
> turn sixty-four, that plan is projected to
> increase by five times the premium, based
> on the current dividends."

After I told that story, Bill Liebler shared one of his own:

I have a friend who I have that same conversation with. "Oh, man,
have you looked at what happened?" I'm like, "Quit looking at that.
It's going to drive you crazy. Quit killing yourself! Unless you're going to rebalance it or do something about it, don't look at it."

Bill then went on to talk about switching from his savings and investing plans to Bank On Yourself.

I think the biggest thing is the ability to leverage your own money in
a way that is very safe and secure. B.O.Y. is a very good vehicle that
allows you to have some predictable growth and then be able to
leverage that money while still getting that growth.

And when you look at buying cars or at doing this or that—
where does the money come from? Well, I either have to pull it out
of savings or investments and pay cash, or I've got to go borrow
money and then somebody *else* is making money on that money.

That's when the lightbulb went on. It just really seemed like a vehicle that lets you live your life and make the kind of decisions you
make every day, knowing that you aren't putting a portion of every
check into a banker's pocket and the rest into the equity of whatever
it is you want to acquire, whether it's a car, or a boat, or a timeshare,
or a long-term investment, like our cabin is for us.

With B.O.Y., that money is going right back in to fund your next project or next purchase.

At the same time, Bill understood how all the myths and misinformation the public has been exposed to about insurance can be hard for some people to overcome.

The insurance wrapper that goes around B.O.Y. has to scare away some people, I'm guessing. But after you read enough and you think about it enough, you understand that this is the only vehicle that gives you such a good deal.

The "Last-Minute" College Funding Alternative

While Bill has a late-arriving child as a good excuse for not thinking about starting a college fund in the early years of marriage, lots of other folks who could have acted well ahead don't face the issue until the time is almost upon them. Tom Snyder, the former Verizon lineman from a previous chapter, is one who didn't start a college fund early—not until his daughter Kelsie was fourteen. Still, he discovered Bank On Yourself just in time.

Kelsie is sixteen now. Two years out, when she's entering college, there's going to be about $35,000 or so in the Bank On Yourself policy. Basically I'll be paying myself back instead of doing it through a conventional bank.

Colleges here are funded heavily by the state, so if she goes to a state college, it's a good bargain. Even if she goes to our best state school, the tuition is only around $5,000 a year.

It may not be adequate if she's going to a school that has a higher tuition, but it will certainly be more helpful than not having anything. And during the four years that she's on campus, the fund will continue to grow.

So even though Tom started late, his Bank On Yourself policy will still make college possible for his daughter.

Granny and Grandpa to the Rescue

College funding doesn't have to be a challenge just for parents and their college-bound children. I want to end this chapter by sharing a page from my personal life.

When our two grandkids were young, Larry and I decided we wanted to help pay for their college educations, while teaching them firsthand how the B.O.Y. process works and giving them a financial head start.

We started B.O.Y. plans for each, when Jake was six and Halle was three.

The plan we set up for Jake is projected to provide about $90,000 for his college education expenses by the time he graduates, based on the current dividends. And Halle's plan is predicted to throw off about $125,000.

Of course, if we use the equity in the plan to finance other things in the meantime and pay back the plans the Spend and Grow Even Wealthier way, there will be even more money in the plans for their education.

Perhaps best of all, we can count on the money not shrinking, even if the stock and real estate markets tumble or go nowhere for the next ten years. We won't wake up in the middle of the night in a cold sweat worrying if the money will be there.

But if either Jake or Halle decides to become an Internet entrepreneur or an actor, musician, writer, film producer, dancer, or artist, and decides not to go to college, the equity could be used to fund their entrepreneurial start-up, to pay for Halle's wedding, or for a substantial down payment on a home. The possibilities are limitless and no one's going to say, "Oh, no—you can't use it for that." It's the "no-strings-attached" way to save for college that comes with all the added benefits of Bank On Yourself.

"We're using B.O.Y. plans to finance college educations for our two grandkids. It's the no-strings-attached way to save for college with all the added benefits of B.O.Y. Our dream for our grandchildren is that they will *never* need to use a bank, finance, or

> credit card company, other than to have
> the convenience of a checking account."

And once Jake and Halle demonstrate they are financially responsible, we'll turn the policies over to them. This will typically (hopefully!) happen when they are twenty-five to thirty years old.

I believe this is the most important financial education any child could have. It will change their lives forever, as it's done for us and so many others.

Our dream for our grandchildren is that they will *never* need to use the services of a bank, finance, or credit card company, other than to have the convenience of a checking account!

CHAPTER 11

Financing Business and Professional Purchases

So far in these pages we've focused on personal uses for Bank On Yourself—as a way of financing your cars, paying off debt, paying for college, providing for retirement, and so on.

Soon after I found out about B.O.Y., I realized it could be used not just for personal finances but for business finances, too. As a business owner myself, I've used this method to finance our business vehicles, as well as to self-finance business equipment that in the past we had been leasing.

If you are a business owner, entrepreneur, or professional, how much do you currently spend leasing or financing vehicles, equipment, office space, or buildings? For some businesses, this can amount to literally hundreds of thousands of dollars or more that they will never see again.

What if, simply by becoming your own
financing source for major business
expenses, you could create a bigger stream
of income in retirement? You could
potentially recapture hundreds of
thousands of dollars—or more—that you
would otherwise never see again.

Now imagine what it would be like to recapture all of those dollars. What would you do with those funds? Expand your business? Add equipment or technology that puts you so far ahead of your competition they may never be able to catch up? Hire that chief operating officer, manager, or executive assistant so you can cut back on your hours and have more time to enjoy your life and family? And what if, simply by becoming your own financing source for major business expenses, you could create a bigger stream of income at retirement?

All of this—and much more—is possible, when you use Bank On Yourself. Let's meet some of the folks who are doing it.

Turning a Love of Horses into a Business

Our journey takes us first to the Arizona desert, home to Susan and Kevin Rowan; perhaps you'll remember them from chapter 9 as the parents of the fourteen- and eighteen-year-old girls who are funding their own B.O.Y. plans. The family lives in what's called a Santa Fe territorial-style house, with the Superstition Mountains providing a dramatic backdrop to the view from their home.

Susan, whom her husband describes as "a short, good-looking girl that likes horses," has a challenging job: for twenty-five years, she has served as a mentor and liaison with teachers of kindergarten through grade twelve who work with learning-disabled youngsters.

Kevin, in his mid-fifties, could be a poster boy for what we think an airline pilot should look like: tall and handsome, commanding, yet with a lighthearted sense of humor. Susan would want me to add that he's an Irishman, with a shock of red hair. When the pair first met, he was a crop duster; after they became a couple, her salary paid for him to accumulate the flying hours he needed to get his Air Transport Rating. Today he's a captain for a major airline. For anyone who cherishes the outdoors, his upbringing sounds nearly ideal.

Kevin:

> I grew up in the Owens Valley of California. My father worked at
> a couple of fish hatcheries—extremely interesting places—and for the
> Department of Fish and Game. We did a lot of arrowhead hunting and
> a lot of fishing. You could pretty much do any kind of outdoor activity
> you wanted without having to go get a landowner's permission.
>
> Financially we never hurt for anything. My parents were pretty
> careful with their money, and they didn't really trust credit that
> much. Anything that you wanted, you better have the money to buy
> it. You didn't go in and leverage yourself to the hilt and buy some-
> thing that you really may not have needed.

Susan's upbringing was very different.

I was a child of a military father, so I was one of what they
call "military brats." We moved every three years of my life.
The last tour was in Germany, and I graduated from a high
school over there. It just enriched me and allowed me to be
free-spirited.

   Then we settled in Yakima, Washington, and I got involved in
the rodeo as one of the princesses for the Toppenish Pow Wow
Rodeo there. We would go tour for parades. And we'd come in for
the grand entrance at rodeos.

   My parents taught us that we needed to save. Once you saw
something you wanted to buy, well, let's research it and make sure
that that's really something that you wanted. You needed to work
toward your goals, and you needed to earn the money.

Kevin:

My parents taught me the principles of using credit wisely, which
was pretty much not using it if you don't need to. But it was lost on
me. My friends and I became children of the '60s.

Jump ahead a few years. Susan and Kevin, now married, were both
becoming concerned about what retirement would be like for them.
Susan, now just three years away from retiring from her teaching job,
had some expansive goals in mind.
Susan:

About six years ago, I started thinking about the retirement income
I'd have, but I didn't feel it was going to be enough to allow us to
have two homes—maybe a home in the desert and a home up in the
mountains—and also be able to travel freely.

Kevin:

I've got 401(k)s with the airlines, and Susan had an IRA and a
few other plans. We took full advantage of those. But we felt we
needed to do something different. You know the old saying that

the definition of insanity is doing the same thing over and over and over again and expecting a different result.

So we decided we needed a different result. There's a newsletter I subscribe to, which is a resource I highly respect and trust and look to for recommendations of ways to make money and grow wealth, as well as what things to stay away from. And it was around then that they had a nice write-up on the B.O.Y. program, and they recommended we check into it. And so I did.

> "The definition of insanity is doing the same thing over and over again and expecting a different result. We decided we needed a different result than we were getting with our 401(k)s and IRAs."

Even with the recommendation, plus reading a report about Bank On Yourself, Kevin still wasn't completely convinced.

I thought, "This is interesting and I'm going to have to try to think of some holes to punch into it." So I'm looking at it from various directions and trying to play devil's advocate. I was trying to find some holes in the theories and the operational effects that I saw in there, and I just really couldn't. I couldn't find a hole. So that's when I decided I'd get a referral to an advisor who could help me set it up right.

He was put in touch with a B.O.Y. Advisor in his area and "we've been at it ever since," he said.

Meanwhile, his wife had already been traveling in a parallel direction. Susan:

I started thinking that I need to have another business after retirement. I grew up around horses and riding horses. Then, after I had my children, I hadn't had horses for a while and I decided I wanted them back in my life. Horseback riding is a great stress reliever for me. That's when I decided to go and get educated on breeding horses, and how to inseminate mares. I began raising brood mares and babies.

Now I've been building this up as a business for four years. I'm working full time in the schools, and, oh my goodness, I'm also the number-one person who cleans up the manure and feeds the horses. It's probably another twenty-five-plus hours a week.

So I'm an ambitious individual who is striving to establish a secondary business for after I retire, and that's raising and breeding quarter horses for the western riding competitions called reining. It's like western dressage.

Kevin:

Here in Arizona, there is an incredible amount of cash flow going into an operation like that, for the start-up and to maintain it. And we grow none of our feed here. We have to buy it all.

To many, one of the most surprising parts of B.O.Y. is how newcomers to the approach can be helped to find the seed money to fund their plans. Perhaps even more surprising is how this can be done while at the same time getting rid of some of the family debt.

Susan:

Our Bank On Yourself Advisor helped us figure this out. He's played such a crucial role in all of this. First educating us and then he's there to counsel and advise us. He looked at the value of our house. We did some refinancing and used the cash to get rid of debt, including about $25,000 of credit card debt and payments we were making on two trucks.

Once we got that debt in check, he told us, "Okay, do you think you could now afford this much to go into Bank On Yourself?" So he was really good leading us into that.

It freed up cash flow so we could then pour money into Bank On Yourself. We started a plan for each of us, and between the two we're putting in $4,000 a month.

We knew that we were still going to have to pump money into the horse business. It costs about $30,000 a year. We draw from our Bank On Yourself policy when we have to. Like when I wanted to upgrade and buy better broodmares, I thought, "Okay, that's a good investment."

The Rowans discussed how they expect the business to be not just self-supporting by the time Susan retires from teaching but to throw off extra retirement income that will allow them to travel and have that second home Susan mentioned. Her husband then talked about the aspects of Bank On Yourself that most strongly appeal to him. Kevin:

To be able to pay yourself back that interest instead of paying it to somebody else—that was probably the hook for me. And just to have the ability to have that money available, so that when you need it, you can get it without having to go down to your banker and make a case for it or go to your credit card company or whatever.

> "The hook for me was paying yourself back instead of someone else. And to have that money available, so you can get it without having to go down to your banker or put it on a credit card."

It seemed to me like it was a very good opportunity to do something for yourself and still do the things that you wanted to accomplish to begin with, instead of having that noose around your neck for the interest and the principal that needs to be paid back.

It's difficult for people to conceptualize an insurance policy where you can put more money in than you need to fund the death benefit. To most people insurance is just a necessary evil. B.O.Y. is outside the box, certainly, but you need to be willing to look beyond the most obvious vehicles for wealth building.

The Rowans now understand that a B.O.Y. life insurance plan can be more than "a necessary evil" and can become a positive factor in one's life and financial planning for the future.

When I asked how their lives might have been different if they'd discovered B.O.Y. ten or twenty years earlier, Susan replied, "I'd already have the mountain place and be doing the traveling, and probably working part time." Kevin's take: "I'd probably not be working."

Turning the Flow of Capital from Cash Out to Cash In

Thirty-something Kris Campbell, like Susan Rowan, grew up as "a military brat" and moved to a different town or different continent every few years. In college she was a voice major learning to sing opera, but after graduation she landed a job as a studio photographer. Eventually that led her into business on her own, doing a unique brand of professional event photography.

Kris Campbell:

> What we do is we go on-site to events, set up a full portrait studio, and print out studio-quality photographs on the spot. We do a lot of proms, graduations, and holiday parties, and we work with corporations on many events.
>
> We also do standard photography so we can go out and take pictures at a convention or other large event and then burn the images to a DVD for the client.

The next thing she said I had to ask her to repeat, because I was sure I hadn't heard her correctly.

> We also print full, four-color photographs onto chocolate.

"So the people *eat* their pictures?" I asked.

> They do! We can print your image in full color onto chocolate lollipops and chocolate CDs. We can even provide them live at events. So we can take your picture and then give you a lollipop with your face on it about five minutes later.

Kris first heard about Bank On Yourself the same way as several other people quoted in these pages.

> I was listening to talk radio and heard that you could redirect the money you're paying to finance companies and the like back to your own pocket. I thought, "I'm paying a lot of money to finance my company." Because of my business, I have a lot of credit cards, and I have a line of credit, and we finance equipment. We finance a lot of things.

I was carrying about $100,000 in debt. So I thought it would be nice if the money was coming back to me rather than going to all those finance companies.

When I asked if she had ever calculated how much she was paying out in interest every month, Kris answered, "I tried *not* to."

Kris started her first B.O.Y. policy with a $21,600 annual premium. The policy was backdated six months—a perfectly legal way for someone to get two years' worth of premiums into their plan in the first six months. This provides a great way to supercharge the cash value in the plan very quickly—so more equity is available, and it's available sooner. In Kris's case, though, for cash-flow reasons she pays her ongoing premiums monthly.

Kris's policy was backdated six months—a perfectly legal way to get two years' worth of premiums into her plan in the first six months, so there's more money available for her to use sooner.

Once she was established with a B.O.Y. policy and in position to take her first loan, she retired a high-interest family obligation.

I used it to pay off my brother and sister-in-law. They had initially loaned me $1,500, at 15 percent interest. I hadn't been paying them anything, because it was an investment for them. It was just sitting there building up interest, and the balance had grown to over $4,000. So I decided to pay it all off.

Aided by a software program, her advisor helped Kris look at different combinations of interest rate and number of months for paying back the loan she took from her Bank On Yourself plan for the $4,000. Most people are happy to let their advisor handle the math and offer alternatives, and Kris did, too. At first. But then, she says, "I ended up getting that software program" so she could juggle the parameters and make loan payback decisions on her own.

My biggest surprise came when Kris started explaining how she was almost immediately able to become her own financing source for an expensive device her personal corporation had been leasing.

My company owed $35,000 on the lease for the piece of equipment that creates the photos on chocolate, and my lease payments were $1,026 a month. I took $35,000 out of my house with what they call a cash-out refinance, and I loaned that money to my company.

Her company paid off the equipment lease, Kris explained, so it owned the equipment outright.

And now my company is paying *me* the $1,026 a month, to pay me back the money I loaned it. I'm now using that money to help fund my Bank On Yourself plan.

So Kris had taken the $35,000 from the refinance and loaned it to her company, and the company had paid off the lease. Every month her company makes a payment to her on the $35,000 loan, and she turns around and puts that money into her policy. She had quickly become her own financing source for a major purchase she had been running through an outside lending institution, while freeing up money to fund her B.O.Y. plan.

I thought that was very creative and resourceful.

Redirecting the finance charges and principal she was paying the leasing company into her own pocket was just a starting point for Kris. She also spends about $20,000 every year on photographic equipment for the business and has now set a goal of financing all that through her policy, too.

All the interest that would just be going down the drain is now going into funding a policy for myself, and it's providing me with life insurance at the same time.

I asked Kris if she realized that she would then also be getting back the full cost of the equipment and supplies she buys each year, in addition to the finance charges she was paying on those costs. She was aware, she assured me. Kris will be able to look at her annual B.O.Y. policy statements and see how she is recapturing both the purchase price and the interest charges over time, along with some extra "profit," when she pays her policy loans back the Bank On Yourself way.

Not surprisingly, when Kris ran the idea of B.O.Y. by some of her business advisors—who, like most people, are ignorant of the facts about the kind of insurance used for B.O.Y. policies—they tried to discourage her.

> I went to a consultant who helps me make decisions in my business, and I told him I had come across this idea about redirecting some of my business debt by using a B.O.Y. policy. He thought I was crazy and told me, "You should never buy that type of life insurance."

Not surprisingly, when Kris ran the idea of B.O.Y. by some of her business advisors (who, like most people, are ignorant of the facts about B.O.Y.), they tried to discourage her.

Some people would have dropped the idea right there. Not Kris; it became clear during our interview that she is a woman who has achieved the level of success she has by keeping an open mind and challenging conventional thinking. (How many photographers would even consider investing $35,000 in equipment that prints edible photos?)

Kris went back to her B.O.Y. Advisor and "put her through the mill. I asked her some tough questions and she was able to answer them all. She has been unbelievably patient with me."

Kris also had been funding a variable universal life policy. After learning about the many advantages of the specially designed type of whole life policy used for B.O.Y., Kris decided her B.O.Y. policy had "better growth potential" and certainly more guarantees. (In fact, the policy Kris had can even lose money and would not be an appropriate type of policy to use for B.O.Y.).

As a result, she decided to "take most of the money I was putting into the other policy each year and put it into my B.O.Y. plan instead."

When I asked Kris what message she hoped readers of this book would take from her story, she didn't skip a beat before replying.

> I would let them know that a lot of people operate their lives like they're victims of circumstances, but you *do* have options to take con-

trol of your financial destiny. You really owe it to yourself to be open to the possibilities out there and find ones that make sense for you.

Businesses and professionals who spend significant sums leasing or financing vehicles, equipment, inventory, or even office buildings will find that all of these expenditures could potentially be financed the B.O.Y. way. The difference this can make over time can be staggering.

You can use B.O.Y. to self-finance business vehicles, equipment, inventory, or even office buildings.

In addition, some business owners may also qualify for tax deductions for interest and depreciation. A knowledgeable tax advisor can provide appropriate guidance. (A referral to a B.O.Y. Authorized Advisor who can do a free, no-obligation B.O.Y. business analysis for you and may also be able to direct you to a CPA in your area familiar with the tax implications of B.O.Y. for business owners and professionals is available at **www.BankOnYourselfFreeAnalysis.com**.)

Leaving the 9-to-5 Rat Race to Become a Real Estate Entrepreneur

Christy and Greg Gammon, introduced in chapter 7, have used B.O.Y. to turn their lives around.
Greg:

> We're both involved in real estate. Christy is a licensed real estate agent; I'm a real estate investor. We flip properties, to use a colloquial term, but we've both been involved in real estate as self-employed individuals for the last couple of years, and we love it. Part of the reason we've been able to do that is due to the success of our Bank On Yourself system.

What's most impressive about what the Gammons are doing is that it provides one more compelling example of leverage. They are taking loans from their policy and using the money not to buy cars or pay off credit cards, but to invest in their business of buying a house, making improvements, and reselling it at a profit—"flipping," as Greg refers to the practice.

A great many Bank On Yourself clients are multiplying the power of their B.O.Y. policies with this double-duty technique—making the same dollars earn for them in two different ways simultaneously.

Christy:

> We've been on a journey with B.O.Y., and we've been able to borrow a lot out of the policies to help us build our business.
>
> Even though we've had some policy loans out, we continue to get the same guaranteed annual cash value increases and we've gotten dividends every year so far, too.
>
> The current investment property that we're working on is about to go on the market, and when it sells, we're about to experience quite a windfall. We're going to be able to pay off our debt for the property and make some larger premium payments into the paid-up additions rider of two of our policies. And then we hope that our next investment will be fully funded by our policies.

They had just sat down a few days earlier and calculated how much they'd already paid in mortgage interest on the property they were about to sell. That cost alone was between $10,000 and $15,000.

Christy:

> That's $10,000 to $15,000 that we could have been putting back into our policies this whole time. Next time that's what we're going to do. We'll use that additional capital we'll be recapturing to invest in more properties.
>
> It's amazing how B.O.Y. starts to really build on itself. That's what's been so exciting for us. We started quite humbly with one residential property that we remodeled and sold. But we have bigger plans and dreams and are looking at maybe expanding into multifamily units, perhaps rentals or even some commercial development.

If we're able to buy our next property purely using our equity in our policies, I cannot wait! That's truly an example of us arriving. That's making the policies work at their full potential.

"We hope our next real estate investment will be fully funded by our policies. I cannot wait! That's truly an example of us arriving."

We're not held back. We can have these dreams because it's already happening. It's going to be possible.

Greg:

The nice thing that we're starting to realize is that we're not beholden to an institution to give us the financial backing that we would need to help our business grow. We're starting to see the fruits of our labors, if you will, in building our policies.

And now we have a very real opportunity to take this money that we've accumulated through the system and use it for our own business purposes immediately.

When we get the windfall from selling this particular property, we're not paying back a financial institution, and all that interest hasn't gone out the window. It's going to continue to build our policies and our business even more.

The success of the Gammons in their real estate adventure is being helped along by another factor. Since they are taking loans from their B.O.Y. policies for a business purpose, the interest portion of their repayments back into the policies may be tax deductible.

These tax deductions may also apply to the interest when you take a loan from your B.O.Y. policy and use the money for a personal investment in stocks, bonds, real estate, a friend's start-up business, or the like. Getting advice from a knowledgeable tax professional is recommended, whether you're taking money for your own business or for a personal business-related investment.

Greg:

Bank On Yourself is the tool that has allowed us to bridge the gap
from "Okay, it's possible" to "Man, this has already happened to us."
It's an amazing realization, when you actually get to the point where
you see it happen.

**Bank On Yourself can also be used
for a variety of charitable and
philanthropic purposes.**

While Christy and Greg can serve as an inspiration to people who
share the longing to go into business for themselves, they provide inspiration in another way, as well. They're an example of one of the
best aspects of the human character: the instinct to help others. Bank
On Yourself can be used for a variety of charitable and philanthropic
purposes, and the Gammons discussed one close to their hearts.

Christy:

So far we've done one trip, a short-term mission to Zambia, Africa,
but we've made a commitment with our church that we would like
to go at least every other year.

We've also sent money ahead to send about seventy children to
school. They were getting meals two to three days a week through a
different program, and we had asked the pastor at our church how
we could help. He said, "Well, there's a village where these children
have access to some food, but they don't go to school."

He looked at our gift and said, "I think this would be perfect to
align with that village, and that would enable the kids to go to
school." So that's our connection with that group, and we plan to be
able to go there every other year to visit with them and bless them.
Of course, they bless us more than they ever know.

We want to have that personal connection versus just sending a
check. Greg has talked with the pastor about economic development
projects and helping people in Zambia be visionary about business
and self-employment and really empower themselves. We're just really excited about what that might hold for us as well.

I'm thirty-three and Greg's forty-two. As we get older, I don't see us needing a whole lot, and we don't see retirement as a time when we're going to be spending more. We're just going to be serving more.

And what's going to make that more possible for the Gammons is the money they will accumulate in the B.O.Y. policies for their retirement. What aspects of B.O.Y. do they credit for this?

Greg:

The thing that comes to mind is the flexibility. It can be tailored to fit your financial situation. It works when you follow the process, and I think that's one of the things that we've really had to learn more than anything else—to just be disciplined to follow the process, and do it faithfully.

We're living the fruits of the labor that we've put into the program, and we really have enjoyed going through this process.

There have been so many side benefits from doing this in terms of the lifestyle changes, the feedback from our children. You can't really put that on paper. It's just one of those things that when you experience it you think, "Man, this is awesome."

CHAPTER 12

Can You Be Too Old to Bank On Yourself?

Just as some people may assume they aren't able to afford a Bank On Yourself program, there are others who assume they're too old to start one. That notion would bring a laugh to the people profiled in this chapter.

A Minister's Legacy for His Children

Reverend Doctor Harry Peatt, the retired minister introduced in an earlier chapter, started his B.O.Y. plan when he turned sixty-seven.

"Doc Hank" grew up in Connecticut and now divides his time between a small town in New England and his winter getaway near a beach in South Carolina. He spoke to me by phone from the South Carolina home, which he described as standing on a double lot at the end of a cul-de-sac near a golf course and featuring a pond that draws ducks and egrets and is "loaded with turtles that I feed every day with stale bread." He has had a career more varied than many. "The biggest inspiration for me," he said, "is my own personal journey."

Doc Hank:

> I've pastored sixteen churches, I've been head chaplain of a state institution, worked for three mental health agencies and as a pastoral counselor. I have a degree from Yale Divinity School and a doctoral degree in pastoral counseling. And I'm also a folk musician.

At six-foot-one and 235 pounds, with a white beard and moustache, Doc Hank exercises regularly and says he carries the weight well but "I have a Santa Claus appearance." He even has what he calls "a state-of-the-art Santa suit" that he dons to "make the rounds on Christmas Eve."

In our conversation, he revealed some very personal details about himself that his jovial manner belies.

Nobody would ever guess that I suffer from depression. As a teen, coming out of surgery on my ankle, an all-A student at Stamford High School, I developed the worst case of depression imaginable. The general opinion was that I had an allergic reaction to the anesthesia. That was at age seventeen. Fifty years later, I still struggle with it at times.

The author William Styron wrote the book *Darkness Visible* about his experience with depression. I think he was sixty years old when it struck him. He was so eloquent. He put into words in a book of less than one hundred pages what everyone who suffers from depression experiences but can't explain to other people.

He wrote, "If I could possibly compare my suffering to any other physical disorder, I would probably be in intensive care, connected up to tubes, getting flowers and cards and visits from people who were very sympathetic and empathetic; and my invalidism would be considered to be valid."

I don't hesitate to talk about my experience, because it helps others who suffer from this.

Sometimes our parents motivate us by providing an example of a kind of life we want to avoid.

My father was not a wealthy man, and my mother was a stay-at-home mom. We didn't live high on the hog, but on the other hand, my father made a decent living. He was a deputy sheriff. I never felt any lack for anything. My father in his youth had to drop out of school early to support his sickly mother. He appeared to me to be an old man, being forty-nine when I was born. He went on from being a prizefighter to wrestling bears in a carnival, and he served in World War I.

When I was in my teens, he would always tell me, "Son, you know I'm getting to be an old man, and I need to count on you to take care of me if I need help." He never had a pension plan and his Social Security was extremely minimal, and I think he thought he was going to be a deputy sheriff for the rest of his natural days. Then

the politics changed when the county went Democratic and he lost
his position. He had virtually no money coming in and had no savings other than the value in his house. I felt like I had to be my parents' savior, so to speak.

It still rings in my mind how my dad would sometimes even start
to cry. It got to the point where he'd have to ask me for a quarter to
go down to the corner store and get a cigar because he was out of
money.

I was at that time a full-time student at Yale Divinity School,
married, and working to pay our bills and my parents' bills. Later on
I always had the thought that I didn't want to put my children in
that position. So I worked my butt off. I never just had one job. I
was a full-time student at Yale and working thirty hours a week for
the postal service, while having a weekend ministerial assignment as
a student minister.

Doc Hank's situation changed virtually overnight at age sixty-four.

I lost my job as the employee assistance program counselor for the
Springfield postal district when they consolidated districts. I still
continued to provide pastoral services to an impoverished little
church. I made a five hundred–mile commute every weekend to do
that, for a weekly salary of $100. Definitely what you'd call a "labor
of love."

I took early Social Security retirement and my church pension,
which gave me enough money to live on. I was always the frugal
type, probably driven a lot by the experience of my childhood. I always had it in the back of my mind that I didn't want to be in the
position my father was, when I got to be his age.

Around that time, Doc Hank's path crossed with a Bank On Yourself Advisor.

I was getting antsy about the stock market, and being in my mid-
sixties at the time, I knew the market can take a big plunge and be
down for seven or eight years. I thought my money would be safer
in B.O.Y. than in the stock market.

I had a lot of trust in my advisor and the clarity of his presenta-
tion and his willingness to take time with me, anytime I had a question while I was contemplating this. I'd hang up the phone and a
day or two later I'd say, "Wait a minute, I've got another question."

Now that I've started my plan, I see that the proof is in the pud-
ding, because when you start getting your first yearly statement and
your second yearly statement, you begin to see the things that you
only had as a concept in your mind.

During his career as a clergyman, Doc Hank had taken out two
whole life plans from a company that served ministers. He'd had
them for twenty-two years, and, although they were traditionally
structured plans that had grown slowly, they had reached a point
where they had a total of over $50,000 in cash value. Unfortu-
nately, however, those policies had no loan value, only a cash sur-
render value. It appeared he had no way to recognize a benefit other
than to die.

His B.O.Y. Advisor found a solution: transfer the cash value into a
new Bank On Yourself plan, as a tax-free exchange.

Immediately after I started my B.O.Y. plan, my death benefit
went from about $70,000 in the two old policies combined, to
about $300,000. That increased to $339,000 after I'd had the new
policy for only one year. And I had access to most of the cash
value *immediately*.

By the time Doc Hank has had his new B.O.Y. policy for just seven
years, it's projected to have a cash value of over $194,000, given the
current dividend schedule, nearly four times what his old policies had
in them. And the total death benefit could increase to over $472,000.

Doc Hank is thinking about using a policy loan to add a second
floor to his garage. The reason is unexpected.

I have a can collection, which is starting to drive me crazy, due to
lack of space. I've got about fifteen thousand beer cans and soda cans
from all over the world, and I have no place to put them, so I want
to build a second story on my garage where it will be my little can
museum.

Doc Hank is planning to use his B.O.Y.
policy for home improvements and
ultimately to provide a legacy for
his children.

Also, the house needs a lot of fixing. I could easily put $100,000 into it, which I would once have had to borrow from a bank. Now, with my B.O.Y. policy, I can borrow from that, instead of a bank. Then I'll be paying that interest back to my own plan and I won't have a monthly payment to worry about.

If I want to borrow money from a bank, they expect "X" amount of dollars every month, or else they can put the heat on you, or foreclose on you. But if I borrow from my B.O.Y. plan at this point, I can go a couple months or a year and not make payments. The worst thing that can happen is that my adoring children would get a little less when I kick the bucket, than if I had paid back all my policy loans.

So if my death benefit was $400,000 at the time, and I had a $50,000 loan outstanding, they'd get close to $350,000. They wouldn't be suffering. They all make more at one job than I ever made with two.

Doc Hank was referring to the fact that if a policy owner dies with loans outstanding, they would simply be deducted from the death benefit, along with any unpaid interest charges.

Wealthy, No Longer Young, But Still Embracing B.O.Y.

Our final visit in these chapters of interviews is to Richard Curtis, a real estate investment officer who started his first Bank On Yourself policy at the age of sixty-one.

Richard:

We were middle class, but my folks did well with what they had, and we never wanted for anything; we never had those types of worries. My father helped put each of us though college. Not that we didn't work to help; all the money that I made summers went

toward my education, so I had a good work ethic. I wasn't afraid
to work.

For the past six years I have worked for a family real estate company that's been in business for going on a century, and as part of
that company I do acquisition work, development work, property
management work. The firm has about ten million square feet across
the country of primarily commercial real estate and industrial-type
property.

Richard's appetite for Bank On Yourself when he first heard about
it was triggered by the notion of an approach in which your principal
and gains are locked in and can't be taken from you because the markets are plummeting. Earlier, he had suffered the kind of painful
financial experience that we all hope will never happen to us or to
anyone we care about.

Some of my speculative real estate ventures worked, and some of
them didn't. A lot depended upon the economy. I was in some partnerships during the late '80s and early '90s that were on the East
Coast. The East Coast went through a real estate depression, so I
lost most of what I had and had to start over. I lost somewhere between $1 million and $2 million.

It hurt. At the time I was pretty devastated, but I just figured I
was still young enough. I always have the attitude that the glass is
half full, rather than half empty, and I have a great background and I
knew I just had to get right back in there and start all over again and
not think about it. That's what I've done.

Like a number of others in these pages, Richard heard about
B.O.Y. via the airwaves.

I listen to a lot of talk radio, and that's where I heard about this.

I was really intrigued by this whole notion that you could fund a
product and then borrow money from it, and through paying yourself back, not have to pay interest to somebody else that you'll never
see again. We all end up paying so much interest on the things that
we buy daily, especially the big-purchase items, like automobiles. In
my case, also boats, plus I own a tractor because I have property east

of here where I have a cabin, that's also a tree farm, so I'm out working in the woods with my tractor there.

Another thing that really interested me was that B.O.Y. is a way
to be able to keep your money growing for you, but if you do need
or want to use part of it to buy another asset, you can do that yourself without having to pay that money back to a bank. You're basically paying yourself back. That was extremely intriguing to me.

I consider myself to be one of those "early adopters," and I'm always looking for new things that others might not necessarily look
at. I'm always intrigued by a new and/or different way to look at
things. When I first heard about B.O.Y., I thought, "Can this really
work?" But when I looked into it, it just made so much sense.

The company my policy is from has paid dividends every single
year, for over one hundred years. It all made sense and it all clicked.

Were there any retirement security concerns that played into
Richard's decision to open a new retirement plan alternative two years
before we spoke, when he was sixty-one?

Although I'll be sixty-five in two years, I want to keep working for a
number of years, partly because I feel I've got so much to give and
there's still so much to do out there. My family has pretty good
genes—my dad's ninety—and I'll probably be out there, as well. So
it's making sure I have enough income to feel comfortable and be set
up right in retirement. I get more conservative as I get older.

Richard started his B.O.Y. plan at sixty-one
to make sure he has enough income to be
"set up right in retirement" and because it
lets him keep his money growing even when
he uses it to buy another asset.

I have a very generous 401(k) from my work. Right now my 401(k)
is not in the market. It's been so volatile. I'm basically in a holding
pattern in a money market at this point.

The difference with Bank On Yourself is that that money is there,
it's readily available. Then when you pay it back, you're paying yourself, but there's flexibility there. It's that flexibility that is not there in

our 401(k) program. And we have very limited investment choices in the 401(k).

Bank On Yourself really gives me the flexible product that other programs do not.

Once my advisor and I got through with the financial assessment, I jumped right in with both feet.

Most of us are not very sophisticated about money. It says a great deal when a man with the money savvy of Richard Curtis carefully scrutinizes Bank On Yourself and decides it's right for him, even though he is already in his sixties.

* * *

Today, many people in their sixties, seventies, and eighties have realized that Bank On Yourself can benefit people of *all* ages. Their reasons for starting B.O.Y. plans are as diverse as wanting to get back the cost of major purchases, protecting their retirement income from volatility, funding college educations for grandchildren, multiplying the dollars they can give to charity, and creating a legacy of financial independence they can pass on for generations to come.

If a person interested in Bank On Yourself turns out to be uninsurable because of health, he or she may still be able to open a B.O.Y. plan. The person being insured doesn't have to be the policy owner; as mentioned earlier, it can be a close relative or even a business associate. Life insurance companies generally have no problem with this arrangement: one person owns the policy but the life insurance coverage is on someone else. What's important is that the person who owns the policy is in control of the money in the policy.

Thanks to this arrangement, being of advanced age is not necessarily a bar to enjoying the benefits of Bank On Yourself.

* * *

It's been said that "if you really want to do something, you will find a way. If you don't, you will find an excuse."

The people who shared their Bank On Yourself journeys in these interviews didn't make excuses. They found a way that has helped them leap ahead financially.

To receive a free, no-obligation Bank On Yourself Analysis that will show you how adding a custom-tailored Bank On Yourself program to your financial plan could help you reach *your* goals and dreams, and to get a referral to a knowledgeable B.O.Y. Authorized Advisor, visit **www.BankOnYourselfFreeAnalysis.com**.

PART FOUR

Setting Out on Your Own Bank On Yourself Journey

If you're tired of gambling with your financial future and—like the people you've been reading about—you're ready to carve out a secure financial future you can predict and count on, you probably have three questions at this point:

How much will it cost to start a B.O.Y. plan that will help me reach my financial goals?

Can I afford it?

How do I find a knowledgeable, qualified advisor to guide me?

I wouldn't think of ending this book without providing you answers to these crucial questions. You'll find them in the final two chapters.

CHAPTER 13

So You're Not Sure You Can Afford It

Always bear in mind that your own resolution to
succeed is more important than any other one thing.
—ABRAHAM LINCOLN

One question I'm often asked is "How much will it cost to start a B.O.Y. plan?" Bank On Yourself Authorized Advisors do not charge fees to prepare an analysis that will show you how much your financial picture could improve with a Bank On Yourself plan, and you are not under any obligation to implement the plan.

If you're convinced the plan will do good things for you, and you decide to implement it, the advisor would receive a commission from the insurance company, which has already been taken into account in the bottom-line numbers you will see in your analysis. Much like buying a flat-screen TV or a couch, *all* the costs of "manufacturing and sales" are already included in the price—or, in this case, in the insurance premium.

However, Bank On Yourself is not one-size-fits-all. Your plan will be custom-tailored to *your* unique situation, and your financial goals and dreams. *So there's no set amount a person must put in to start a plan. You can begin at whatever level is comfortable for you.*

Many people are surprised to discover how easy it is to find the dollars to start on the new financial road described in these pages. Think back to the people who shared their stories for this book: many of them were in debt or feeling financially pinched and yet, guided by a B.O.Y. Advisor, were soon enjoying the experience of being on the road to financial security.

In many cases this came about through changes in their fixed expenses that freed up cash flow for their new Bank On Yourself plans, with little or no increase in their monthly out-of-pocket cost.

Will that be possible for you? Like many of the folks profiled here, I think you'll find it encouraging to know how many places there are to find the "seed money" to fund your plan. You don't need to be an oil baron or well off to Bank On Yourself. It's possible to start with a small monthly amount. So don't make the mistake of thinking that your financial situation, however bleak it may seem, will keep you from becoming a happy Bank On Yourself success story.

On the other hand, like many of those interviewed here, you may be surprised by the creative ways a Bank On Yourself Advisor can guide you to funding a bigger plan than you thought possible, sooner than you thought possible.

But if, like many people, you don't typically have a pile of extra cash lying around at the end of the month, how can you possibly afford to get started with a Bank On Yourself plan? Here are the most common answers that make it possible:

The Eight Most Common Ways to Find the Money to Start Your B.O.Y. Plan

1. Restructure debt

Many people are surprised to discover how readily a B.O.Y. Advisor finds ways they can reduce their monthly expenses so that they can easily afford to start a plan.

In some situations, the answer lies in cleverly reducing debt and using the dollars freed up for Bank On Yourself. Remember Susan and Kevin Rowan, the horse breeder and airline pilot you read about in chapter 11? They replaced the mortgage on their home with a new one that gave them some cash in hand. They used this cash to pay off the loans on two trucks and all of their credit card debt. That freed up a significant amount of monthly cash flow to help them fund their first two B.O.Y. plans.

You've read the story (in chapter 8) of Dr. Jerry West. Because you have the option of paying the premium monthly, quarterly, semiannually, or annually, if you choose to pay an annual premium, you'll have more cash value available to you sooner. Jerry soon took a policy loan, which he used to pay off the loan on his car. With no more monthly car payments to make to an outside finance company, he was able to use those dollars to make the loan payments to his B.O.Y. policy instead.

Even better, this new arrangement allowed him to jump-start the process of becoming his own source of financing for his cars so he could start getting back the cost of those cars and recycle those dollars to buy future cars.

One way to free up cash flow might seem surprising at first glance: if you're trying to reduce credit card balances by paying more than the minimum each month, consider stopping. You may come out ahead paying only the minimums and putting the extra amounts into a B.O.Y. plan. Case in point: a B.O.Y. client from the Midwest who was in his fifties was paying $600 to $800 a month more than the minimum payment due on his credit cards. You might think continuing to eliminate that debt as quickly as possible would be his best option.

If you're trying to reduce credit card balances by paying more than the minimum each month, consider stopping. You may come out ahead paying only the minimums and putting the extra amounts into a B.O.Y. plan.

However when his B.O.Y. Advisor ran an analysis, he discovered that if the man cut back to the minimum payment due and put the difference into a B.O.Y. plan instead, he would have a nest egg worth around $50,000 *more* when he retires at sixty-five.

In a typical situation, there might be enough in the B.O.Y. plan in just a few years to take a policy loan and pay off all credit card debt in one fell swoop. By repaying the loan to your policy, you'd then start recapturing the interest you were paying to the credit card companies, along with a portion of the purchase price of the items you initially paid for by credit card.

You will often come out ahead this way, whether you're paying $100 or $1,000 more than the minimum due.

Others have used a home equity line of credit to consolidate and pay off higher interest rate credit cards.

2. Reduce funding of your 401(k) or other retirement plans

A number of the people interviewed for the book found money to finance their B.O.Y. plan by backing off on funding their 401(k) or other retirement accounts and continuing to pay only the amount that their employer matches.

This brought them the guarantees, tax advantages, and flexibility a B.O.Y. plan provides that their traditional, government-sponsored 401(k), IRA, or pension plan does not. They've been able to stop playing retirement-plan poker and have the peace of mind that a predictable retirement income stream brings.

This was a path chosen by Tom O'Brien (chapter 9), who dropped his annual 401(k) contribution from $20,000 a year to the $1,200 his employer matched. Dick Nelson (chapter 7), who did the same thing, said he wanted to have a "secure retirement" and "a guaranteed income coming for a specific length of time."

Also in chapter 7, when advertising account executive Alan Twelkemeier decided to strike out on his own, he rolled over the funds in his retirement account into a type of annuity that would then pay out $3,000 for each of the next six years—money that pays the premium for his B.O.Y. plan during that time.

3. Raid your IRA or 401(k)

Early retiree Tom Snyder (chapter 7) used a federal plan, the 72(t), to pull money out of his traditional retirement plan, which he then used to fund his B.O.Y. plan. This enabled him to avoid the usual premature distribution penalty anyone younger than fifty-nine and a half would otherwise be required to pay. (If you want to consider this route, be sure to consult with a qualified advisor and tax professional.)

4. Tap your savings

Lisa Sabo, the administrative assistant whose story appears in chapter 9, had been building an emergency fund by contributing regularly to a money market account. Once she understood how a B.O.Y. plan can also serve as an emergency fund, she opened a plan and moved her money market funds into it. That was a much better place for the money, she decided, "as opposed to having it just sit in something that's taxable and making practically nothing."

Similarly, the O'Briens, who had been pouring money into various savings and investment accounts, sold off $60,000 of mutual funds to finance their first four B.O.Y. plans.

A solid financial plan must be built on a stable foundation of savings with little or no exposure to risk. This includes cash and so-called cash equivalents, such as CDs, treasuries, money market funds, bonds, and life insurance. You may have heard the rule of thumb that says a percentage of your assets equal to your age should be in safe vehicles. So, by that measure, a fifty-year-old should have 50 percent of her assets safely tucked away.

Moving some of your safe money into a B.O.Y. plan means dollars working much harder for you, without losing sleep.

Moving some of your safe money into a B.O.Y. plan means dollars working much harder for you, without losing sleep.

---

5. Rethink that tax refund

Some people love getting a big tax refund check in the mail every year. But that's your own money you're getting back. You're giving the government an interest-free loan, while getting a zero rate of return on your money. It's fast and easy to adjust your withholding, immediately increasing your monthly cash flow (in some cases by hundreds of dollars a month), and you could then use those dollars to fund a bigger B.O.Y. policy.

6. Make lifestyle changes

Remember Alice Englund, whose story appears in chapter 2? She told me she started her first plan by holding on to her car a few years longer than she normally would have.

Christy and Greg Gammon (chapters 7 and 11) were surprised at how easily they were able to cut their monthly costs by simple changes such as eating out less and bundling their Internet, cable TV, and phone services. These changes helped them achieve their goal of becoming their own bosses so they could set their own hours and spend more time with their two sons.

As a result of these lifestyle changes, the Gammons were able to put $1,000 a month into their first B.O.Y. plan. Did they feel deprived? Not at all. According to Christy, "It actually felt really good. It felt like we were making the best decisions for our family, and we knew it was going to enable us to be more active and involved parents in our boys' day-to-day lives."

7. Convert existing life insurance policies

Chapter 12 told how the Reverend Doctor Harry Peatt was able to kick-start his B.O.Y. plan by transferring the cash value from two old whole life policies that had no provision for taking loans. The $50,000 of cash value he moved into his B.O.Y. plan, as a tax-free exchange, skyrocketed his death benefit immediately by over 400 percent and gave him access to most of the cash value almost immediately. And it's projected that just seven years after starting his plan, he'll have nearly *four times* the cash value his old plans had taken twenty-two years to reach. (A word of caution: giving up an old insurance policy may not be in your best interest. A Bank On Yourself Advisor can explain the pros and cons and show you the short- and long-term impact of doing this.)

Transferring cash value from existing policies can work whether you have whole life policies, universal life policies, variable life policies, or certain other types of life insurance. In some situations, taking a withdrawal from the old policy and using that to fund a B.O.Y. plan may be an option.

Kris Campbell, the photographer introduced in chapter 11, redirected a portion of the premium she was paying on a variable universal life policy into a B.O.Y. policy, because B.O.Y. comes with guarantees other types of policies don't. And in some cases, it can work in your favor to give up term insurance policies that will ultimately become too expensive to keep and direct those premiums into a B.O.Y. plan. You may even end up with a similar or larger death benefit this way.

8. Manage your home equity wisely

Many people like the feeling of security that comes with building up equity in their home, or owning it free and clear. Some people make extra mortgage payments, or refinance to a fifteen-year mortgage, even if it makes them feel financially pinched.

In recent times, we've learned the hard way that there are dangers to having too little equity in your home. But there are also hidden dangers to having too much equity in your home. Unfortunately, most people never discover these pitfalls until it's too late. How can having extra equity in your home be a *bad* thing? Let's look at the facts:

* Payments of principal you make into your home do not make money for you. Is your home going to appreciate at a different rate depending on whether you owe $200 or $200,000 on your mortgage? Of course not. When you go to sell your home, it won't be worth a single penny more if you've paid your mortgage down, or paid it off. Which means the money you sink into your home isn't working for you at all. Your equity is earning you a *zero* percent rate of return!

However, money you put into your Bank On Yourself policy grows continuously. And as you understand by now, you can borrow your cash value from the policy, invest it elsewhere, or use it for anything you want, and still have it working for you. In fact, you could use the equity in your policy to pay off your mortgage, if you really wanted to, and your policy would continue to grow as though you never borrowed a dime.

* The equity in your home is not liquid. This is a key consideration. Have you thought about how you'll get your hands on the equity in your home if you need or want it? You may be able to refinance or take out a home-equity loan. However, if you lose your job or become disabled, you probably won't be able to qualify for a re-fi or a loan; your money will be *locked up* in your home.

What do you think your mortgage banker is going to say if you become disabled or lose your job, and you beg him to give you a break because you made all those extra payments, or because you demonstrated how responsible you are by paying your mortgage over fifteen years instead of thirty? All that begging and a quarter won't even buy you a cup of coffee. Your next payment is *still* going to be due—in full—in thirty days. And if you can't make your payments for ninety days, the bank will foreclose on you, probably meaning you'll lose *all* the equity you sweated so hard to build up in your home.

An acquaintance of mine found this out the hard way. After being out of work for eight months when his company downsized, he was unable to make his mortgage payments. He had regularly made extra payments on his mortgage, but that made no difference. The bank foreclosed; he lost the house and all the equity he had in it, including those extra payments, and he had a black mark on his credit report for years, which up to then had been impeccable.

As Mark Twain noted, "A banker is a fellow who lends you his umbrella when the sun is shining, but wants it back the minute it begins to rain."

As Mark Twain noted, "A banker is a fellow who lends you his umbrella when the sun is shining, but wants it back the minute it begins to rain."

A lot of folks rely on home equity lines of credit. Unfortunately, having a home equity line of credit is no guarantee you'll have access to money when you want or need it: millions of people got a real shock when they received letters from their bank informing them that because the value of their home had fallen, their credit line was slashed. Or frozen.

The other way to get at the equity in your home is to sell your house. However, you may be in for an unpleasant surprise, because . . .

* **The equity in your home is not guaranteed.** Real estate values go up, but they also go down, a painful reality that came as an unhappy surprise to many people in the real-estate bust of 2007–2009, as at many times in the past.

In addition, you have no guarantee that the market will be up when you're ready to sell, and you have no way of knowing how long it will take to sell.

* **There is no tax benefit to having equity in your home.** You get a tax break for the interest that you pay, but *not* for your payments of principal. The faster you pay your mortgage down, the less interest you'll pay, and the lower your tax benefit. Given that this is the only real tax break consumers get for paying interest, why give it up if there's a better alternative?

If I told you I had a great investment for you that has *no* growth, *no* guarantees, *no* tax break, and *no* liquidity, how much of it would you want?

> If I told you I had a great investment for you that has *no* growth, *no* guarantees, *no* tax break, and *no* liquidity, how much of it would you want? The downside of reducing your mortgage balance quickly is hardly ever talked about.

Described that way, building a lot of equity in your home doesn't sound like such a good deal, does it? But that's the problem: the downside of paying off your mortgage quickly is hardly ever talked about. And it breaks my heart that so many well-intentioned people are trying to pay off their mortgage faster, often while struggling to pay bills each month and carrying credit card balances and other debt.

On the other hand, a Bank On Yourself policy will grow by a guaranteed rate every year, your equity is liquid (you can get your hands on it whenever you want or need it and no credit application is ever required), and it comes with the tax advantages we covered earlier.

And, even though my husband and I have used the equity in our policies to purchase and finance numerous big-ticket items, including our cars, a home theater, luxury timeshares, fine art, and unexpected medical bills, we still have enough equity in our plans to pay off our mortgage in full today if we choose to!

Added bonus: as you now know, if we did borrow from our policies to pay off our mortgage, those policies would continue growing as though we'd never borrowed a dime.

Before we really understood all the advantages that building equity in our Bank On Yourself policies has over building it in our home, we were very seriously considering refinancing to a fifteen-year mortgage. But instead we refinanced with a thirty-year mortgage so the equity in our home increases at a slower rate. This maximized our tax deduction and gave us flexibility and peace of mind.

We're putting the difference between what our monthly payment would have been if we'd gone the route of a fifteen-year mortgage, and the lower payment we ended up with, into a Bank On Yourself policy. Over time, we'll end up with far more wealth than if we had plowed that money into our home. Plus, knowing we have the ability to pay off our home anytime we want, using the equity in our B.O.Y. plans, makes us feel much more secure and in control than having our money locked up inside our home.

Please understand I'm *not* suggesting you use your home equity to directly finance your lifestyle, or that you use your home as an ATM, as it's been referred to in recent years. This will *not* get you the desired result. But you may find that you can restructure your mortgage, or stop making extra payments of principal, and free up more seed money to help fund your Bank On Yourself plan so you can move closer to a secure financial future.

*   *   *

Here's a little experiment to determine how you could benefit from Bank On Yourself to change the flow of money in your life from cash *out* to cash *in*.

The best way to illustrate how you can benefit from this powerful way to grow wealthy by running your major purchases through a B.O.Y. plan, instead of financing them or paying cash for them, is to look at real numbers—*your* numbers.

Do you know how many dollars are now leaving your home— never to be seen again—that could be recaptured when you Bank On Yourself? Sit down at your computer or grab your calculator and let's find out what the number will be over the next thirty years.

I've shown you how you could have a *much* larger nest egg, without taking on risk or losing sleep, simply by financing your cars through a B.O.Y. plan. Cars are the second-largest lifetime expense for most Americans after their homes, so let's start there.

(The car loan illustration in chapter 2 was based on purchasing a $30,000 car with financing at an interest rate of 7.5 percent. Recall that the interest charges for the entire four years of the loan total $4,800, which is 16 percent of the price of the car. For consistency, I've used the same 16 percent figure in the following example.)

Determining How You Could Benefit from Bank On Yourself

If you typically finance your cars . . .
How many cars will your household buy over
the next thirty years?   _____
Multiply your answer to the above question by
the average cost of your cars after any trade-in: $_____
Multiply the last number by 16 percent, to find
the typical total amount you'll pay in interest
over the *life* of each loan (see note above): $_____
Add together the last two numbers to get
your total cost for your cars over thirty years: $_____

If you typically lease your cars . . .
Multiply your annual lease payments by the number
of cars your family leases, then multiply by thirty years: $_____
Multiply the average amount you pay upfront for
each car lease by the number of cars you expect to
lease over the next thirty years: $_____
Add the two numbers to get your total cost: $_____

The numbers add up very quickly, don't they? Now imagine what you'd do with all that money, if you were able to get it all back (and then some) in a B.O.Y. plan.

If you typically pay cash for your cars . . .
Remember, you finance *everything* you buy—you either *pay* interest to others to use their money or you *give up* the interest and investment income you could have earned on your money, had you invested it instead of paying cash. You'll also pay taxes on the growth in a regular savings, money market, or investment account.

Recall from chapter 2 what happens when you save money in a regular savings account to pay cash for major purchases like cars (Figure 1).

As you can see, this method of paying for cars isn't going to throw off much of a retirement income, unlike a Bank On Yourself plan, which credits you the exact same cash value increase and dividend, regardless of whether you've borrowed your equity to buy things.

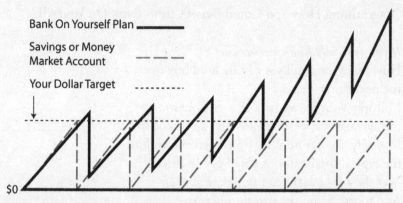

Figure 1—Comparison of growth in B.O.Y. versus savings account

And what about vacations?

How much do you spend on average on your vacations? $_____

Multiply that number by the number of vacations

you think you'll take over the next thirty years: $_____

I'm giving you a break here, because I'm not going to

ask you to include how much you'll spend *financing*

your vacations over the next thirty years.

Now add that last number to the total cost you

came up with for your cars: $_____

This total is the amount of money that's *going* to leave your home over the next thirty years, just for cars and vacations alone!

Painful, isn't it? Perhaps I should have told you to grab a bottle of Pepto-Bismol before we started.

If you didn't bother to do the arithmetic yourself, I'll provide answers that are fairly typical for an average family (see table on next page).

Should I keep going? Because we haven't even touched on what's flying out of your pocket for home improvements, college educations, a second home, a boat or RV, business equipment, country club initiation fees. . . .

I'm hoping that by now the message is clear: you may never get out of financial prison or win the money game if you keep doing things the way you've been doing them. And the financial hole you've been digging yourself into will only get deeper.

Yet people focus most of their time and effort on chasing after higher returns on their savings and retirement accounts. After all, isn't

Cost of Cars and Vacations Over Thirty Years for a Typical Family:

Cost of cars over thirty years

Two $25,000 family cars (after trade-in value), every four years for thirty years, which (rounded off) is 14 cars × $25,000	$350,000

+ Finance charges

Multiply $350,000 by 16 percent (the typical amount you'll pay in interest over the *life* of each loan) to calculate the total finance charges	$ 56,000

Total cost for cars over thirty years	**$406,000**
Cost of vacations over thirty years: $2,500 × 30	$ 75,000
Total cost of cars and vacations over thirty years	**$481,000**

that what all the financial advisors, stockbrokers, magazines, TV, and other media tell you to do?

But how much of a bump-up in percentage points can you really hope to get? Will it really make all that much difference in the long run? Do you have the emotional constitution to stomach the increased risk that inevitably comes with higher returns?

How does that compare with the rate of return you'll get when you recapture every dollar you pay for major purchases?

When you consider how much money is leaving your home in both principal and interest payments every year, doesn't it make sense to focus time, energy, and money on recapturing and leveraging dollars that would otherwise be lost forever?

Then you could use those dollars to fund a rock-solid retirement plan, and your hard-earned money would continue to grow in *all* markets—the good, the bad, and the ugly. You'll be able to stop gambling with your financial future and gain control of your money and finances.

All this can happen by simply running your major purchases through a Bank On Yourself plan, or a system of B.O.Y. plans you set up over time, as many of those who shared their B.O.Y. journeys with us are already doing. It's easier than you might think, and the sooner you start, the sooner you'll reap the rewards.

Some people who buy a car only every ten years or so, rarely take vacations, and live a sparing lifestyle wonder if they would still benefit from B.O.Y. The answer is yes. After all, *every* dollar you *do* spend on major purchases could be recaptured in your B.O.Y. plan, where it can go to work for you growing your nest egg predictably and without the volatility of the stock and real estate markets.

You can receive substantial benefit from B.O.Y. *even* if you live a spartan lifestyle and buy cars or take vacations infrequently.

And once you realize that buying things like cars and taking vacations the Spend and Grow Wealthy way can grow your nest egg, rather than drain it, you just might start giving yourself permission to enjoy a few more of life's luxuries without feeling guilty, as a number of the people who told their stories in chapters 7 through 12 discovered.

The final chapter tells you how to take the next step and where to get expert help to make sure your new plan will grow as quickly as possible and will help you reach as many of your goals and dreams as possible.

CHAPTER 14

Getting Started

*If you do what you've always done, you will get what
you've always gotten.*

—ANONYMOUS

I hope this book has helped open your mind to a powerful, proven wealth-building method—one that has given my own family, and some 100,000 other individuals and families, the financial peace of mind most people seek. If it has, you're probably wondering what to do next to get started and where to look for expert help. You'll find the answers to those questions here.

You know by now that I believe Americans have been brainwashed into believing that we must accept risk, volatility, and unpredictability to grow a sizable nest egg and a comfortable lifestyle in retirement. We've also been misled and misinformed about what may well be the safest and most powerful financial vehicle ever created.

But you've been reading about people of all ages and incomes and from all walks of life who found a way to build wealth and financial security using the Bank On Yourself method. Simply by following the program described in these pages, the following advantages could be yours, too. Please check the ones that are of greatest importance to you:

☐ You could look forward to a retirement income you can predict and count on
☐ You could receive a guaranteed annual cash value increase every year, along with the potential for annual dividends that, although not guaranteed, have been paid every single year for over one hundred years by the insurance companies used by Bank On Yourself Authorized Advisors

☐ You could be free from worries that your principal will lose value if there's a stock or real estate market downturn, and you'd have the security of knowing that, once credited to your policy, neither your annual guaranteed cash value increase nor any dividends you may receive can be taken away—they are locked in

☐ You could know in advance both your minimum guaranteed annual increase and the minimum annual income you could take from your plan, so you *don't* have to pin your hopes for a secure financial future on luck, skill, or guessing games

☐ You would remain in control of your equity in the plan, to use when and how you choose, without the restrictions or penalties common to 401(k)s and other government-sponsored retirement plans

☐ By running your major purchases through the plan instead of using bank financing, leasing, or credit cards or paying cash, you could get back the entire cost and recapture interest you'd otherwise pay and never see again

☐ By using a combination of policy loans and dividend withdrawals, as described in these pages, you may be able to take a retirement income with little or no tax consequences, as long as current tax laws remain unchanged

☐ You could leverage your money by having the same funds at work for you in two ways at the same time

☐ You could have a plan that has an income tax–free death benefit, providing peace of mind for your family or heirs, if you were to pass away before you finished funding the plan

🔑 Key Concept

No other savings, financial planning, or retirement planning method—at least none I've ever heard of—can offer this combination of growth, guarantees, and protection. Not stocks, or bonds, or CDs, or real estate, or mutual funds, or gold, or commodities, or currency.

The ways you can use Bank On Yourself to improve your life are almost without number. Here are just a few that are represented by the experiences of some of the people featured in this book:

Turn the Flow of Money from Cash Out to Cash In

If you did the little experiment at the end of the last chapter, you already know how much money will leave your home over the next thirty years, just for your family's cars and vacations. For the average family, it's close to half a million dollars. That's a real eye-opener, especially when you realize that simply by running those purchases through a B.O.Y. plan—or a system of B.O.Y. plans—all of those dollars you now pay in both principal and interest charges could come back to you (and then some) to help finance a secure retirement for you.

In many cases this could result in a nest egg *several* times larger than you'd have if you saved for retirement the traditional ways. All without the nail-biting, roller-coaster ups and downs, and sleepless nights.

Knowing you're getting back the cost of those purchases gives you more freedom to enjoy them. Want to take that trip you've been putting off to the Mexican Riviera, with all the frills, like Alan Twelkemeier? Go ahead and take it, guilt-free! Want more time with your children? Remember Gene Pittman, who used his B.O.Y. plan to pay for the backyard swimming pool that became a magnet for his young son's friends, giving Gene more companionship time with his son? The world is a different place when you realize you don't have to choose between enjoying life's luxuries or saving for tomorrow.

Use Your Money and Still Have It Work for You

One unique and powerful benefit of a B.O.Y. plan is that if it's from one of a handful of companies that offer this feature, you can borrow from the plan and invest the money in anything you want. Because your plan continues to grow at the same rate, regardless of any loans you take, your money can do double duty for you. This may be the ultimate financial leverage, making your dollars earn for you in two different ways simultaneously.

Create an Emergency Fund for Peace of Mind

While on your way to your other goals, you can create a cash reserve you can use for almost any emergency—to fix or replace that broken air conditioner when the temperature hits the 90s, to cover unreimbursed medical expenses, which typically cause 50 percent of all bankruptcies, to allow you to take time off to help out family members in need, or to cover living expenses if you get laid off or injured and can't work for a while.

For example, my massage therapist had to have both wrists operated on for carpal tunnel syndrome. On discovering she wouldn't be able to work for at least four months, she took a $10,000 loan from her B.O.Y. plan. She was amazed and relieved to find she had that much equity and wouldn't have to max out her credit cards.

You can skip some payments on your policy loans and no one is going to make intimidating collection calls, repossess your things, or foreclose on you. No late fees and no credit applications to fill out. No begging for a loan, no embarrassment and frustration of being turned down. It's your money to use as you wish.

Build a College Fund

When you Bank On Yourself to finance a college education, you can avoid the mistake most parents make of paying for college with funds that could have gone to enrich their retirement, or by saddling their children with tens of thousands of dollars of debt by the time they finish college.

And, unlike one standard savings plan used by parents—the 529 plan—if the child doesn't end up going to college or qualifies for a scholarship, the money you had earmarked for college can be used at any time and for anything you desire. There are no restrictions or penalties, because with B.O.Y., you're in control.

Finance Business and Professional Expenses

B.O.Y. works for business as well as personal expenses, so you could recapture the cost of company vehicles, equipment, even office buildings, or use your equity to start or expand a business. You may also qualify for tax deductions for interest and depreciation, in addition to all the other advantages of B.O.Y.

* * *

The Bank On Yourself Challenge

No one has been able to come forward with information on any other financial product or vehicle that does all the above things, other than the one you've been reading about in these pages: Bank On Yourself. A substantial cash reward still waits for the first person who can show they use a different product or strategy that can match or beat the many advantages and guarantees of B.O.Y. Care to take the Challenge? Visit the Web site **www.BankOnYourself .com**.

* * *

Don't Settle for Substitutes

When your plans are designed by a B.O.Y. Authorized Advisor, they can provide you with *all* of the following advantages:

> They are dividend-paying whole life policies from companies that have paid dividends every single year for at least the past one hundred years in a row and are among the top life insurance companies in terms of financial strength, according to independent rating services

> They are non–direct recognition companies, which means they credit you the exact same dividend even when you've taken loans from your plan

> The policies are structured to include a paid-up additions rider (PUAR), the piece of the puzzle that's like putting the growth of your plan on legal steroids

> The PUAR is very flexible, so you can pay that portion of the premium how and when you want, and you can make partial payments or skip payments and be able to make up for them later. In addition, you can typically withdraw your paid-up additions and put them back in later

Out of over 1,500 life insurance companies, only a handful meet all of these requirements.

A Word of Caution

When you're ready to get started, how do you find someone qualified to design and implement your Bank On Yourself plan? You may be tempted to discuss what you've learned from this book with your financial advisor or to show him a copy of this book and ask him to help you implement this program.

But this book was written for "regular folks," not for financial advisors. It takes most advisors months or even a year of advanced training to understand the full technical details and ins and outs of Bank On Yourself. Anyone who's not a financial advisor would be bored by all that technical information.

If you talk to a financial advisor or insurance person who has not thoroughly investigated the little-known type of policy used for B.O.Y., or who is not familiar with the proper way to structure the policy or use it to get back the cost of major purchases, here's what he is likely to tell you:

1. *"You should never buy that kind of life insurance."*
By now you understand that most advisors were never trained on this type of life insurance policy and don't understand what a paid-up additions rider is or how to use it to turbo charge the growth of the plan.

They got their training the same place Suze Orman, Dave Ramsey, and 99.9 percent of all advisors got it, and don't have a clue how a Bank On Yourself policy is different.

2. *"It's a good idea, but you should use a different type of policy, like a universal life, equity-indexed universal life, or a variable life policy."*
No other life insurance product comes with as many guarantees as whole life, and it is the *only* one recommended for Bank On Yourself.

Also, some advisors will try to steer you toward a different product because their contracts require them to use only certain companies.

3. "It sounds too good to be true—you can't get back the cost of major purchases and use that money to fund your retirement."

I hope this book has shown you it's entirely possible to do that, and you've heard from many folks who are already doing it. It's not taught in schools or universities, and it requires a major shift in thinking from what we've been taught about money and financing. It's something almost anyone can do. B.O.Y. is not a magic pill and it won't happen overnight, but if you have a little patience and discipline, it will soon turn your financial life around and give you peace of mind.

4. "Oh, I can help you do that."

If your advisor doesn't have specialized training in properly structuring a B.O.Y. plan and how to use it to get back the cost of major purchases, or he uses the wrong company or product, your plan could grow much more slowly or you could lose some of the tax advantages, or both. Unfortunately, most advisors "don't know what they don't know" about Bank On Yourself. You've undoubtedly heard the saying "A little knowledge can be a dangerous thing," and in my experience, that's often true in the case of B.O.Y.

And if your advisor tells you he already understands all the important details necessary to help you implement and benefit from B.O.Y., you may want to ask him, "If you *could* have done this for me, why *didn't* you?"

So Where Do You Find Expert Help?

Requests from folks all over the country for a referral to a financial advisor who understands all the ins and outs of the B.O.Y. method and could act as their professional guide led to the creation of the Bank On Yourself Authorized Advisor Program. There was a need for training financial advisors and insurance agents interested in mastering this little-known kind of life insurance. Much of the training focuses on how the advisor can coach his or her clients through the years to become their own source of financing—ultimately for their entire lifestyle.

Today, there are some two hundred highly qualified professionals across the United States and Canada who form the core of Bank On Yourself Authorized Advisors. In addition to working with the special kind of life insurance companies recommended for B.O.Y., each is also a licensed financial advisor or life insurance agent who has undergone hundreds of hours of additional training on the technical aspects of the features that make these policies such a powerful financial tool.

They have passed a certification test, take continuing education classes, and work under the guidance of B.O.Y. technical and policy-design experts who have each designed at least two thousand B.O.Y. plans. For a referral to a Bank On Yourself Authorized Advisor who can design a custom-tailored plan to help you reach your goals and dreams, go to **www.BankOnYourselfFreeAnalysis.com**.

If You're Tired of Hoping and Praying for Financial Peace of Mind . . .

As I write this in late 2008, the Dow and S&P 500 are back where they were ten years ago. Most investors would have made just as much and slept like a baby if they'd stuffed their money inside their mattresses.

In chapter 3, we learned why investors don't even come close to equaling the long-term returns of the overall stock market and that, in fact, over the past twenty years, the average investor's rate of return—at best—*barely* outpaced inflation. One category of investors' returns was so poor it actually *lagged* inflation by 1.49 percent per year!

Another thing to consider: what if history repeats itself and it turns out we're in another lengthy go-nowhere stock market cycle, as discussed in chapter 3, and you wake up a decade from now to find yourself right back where you were in 1998? How would that affect the plans for your financial future and retirement?

We've always thought we could depend on the value of our homes to help supplement our retirement income. Yet, long-term, the value of houses has increased an average of only 1 percent a year, after adjusting for inflation, as we learned in chapter 1. Given this fact, it might be worth rethinking how much you can count on your home equity to fund your retirement.

In recent years, desperate to make up for lost time, many people have tried to cash in on the latest hot investment, oblivious to the historical ups and downs and volatility of these investments. Gambling and speculating with our future has replaced saving and building a strong financial foundation.

> Today's hot investment is almost always tomorrow's loser. Falling victim to the "but this time is different," or "this investment can't go down," or "I'll know when to get out" mentality is a sure path to financial *insecurity*.

Bank On Yourself is not a magic pill, as I've noted here. I don't believe there *are* any magic pills.

But what I *do* know is that B.O.Y. provides a long-term solution to a long-term problem. And the only regret expressed by those who shared their journeys here was that they didn't find out about B.O.Y. sooner.

So it comes down to how you answer these questions:

1. Would you like to know what your nest egg will be worth in ten, twenty, or thirty years, or whenever you plan to use it?
2. Would you like to be able to substantially increase the size of your nest egg, without worrying about the ups and downs of stocks, mutual funds, real estate, and other volatile investments, simply by running your major purchases through a Bank On Yourself plan?
3. Would you like to look forward to opening your plan's annual statements because they always contain good news and never any ugly surprises?
4. Would you like to enjoy more of life's luxuries guilt-free, because you know you can do that without robbing your nest egg?
5. Would you like to leap ahead financially, gain control of your money and your finances, have the sheer joy of beating the banks and finance companies at their own game, and win the money game?

If your answer to one or more of these questions is yes, then I hope you'll take the logical next step and investigate what B.O.Y. can do for *you*. It's not too late to rescue your financial plan, but don't put it off another day. It's easy to find out the bottom-line results you could achieve through a Bank On Yourself plan, custom-tailored to your unique financial situation, goals, and dreams. Simply go to **www.BankOnYourselfFreeAnalysis.com** and enter the information requested, and you will be put in touch with a Bank On Yourself Authorized Advisor. Or you can use the Analysis Request Form at the back of this book.

To request a free, no-obligation Bank On Yourself Analysis that will show you how you could benefit from a program tailored to your goals and dreams, go to www.BankOnYourselfFreeAnalysis.com or complete the request form at the back of this book.

In about an hour, the B.O.Y. Advisor can do an analysis that will show you how much your financial picture could improve, if you added B.O.Y. to your financial plan. There will be no high pressure and, in fact, you will not be asked to buy anything at this meeting. The analysis is *free* and there's *no* obligation.

If you're concerned about where you'll find the money to fund your plan, a B.O.Y. Advisor may be able to show you ways to do that, as I explained in the previous chapter.

And if you wish to verify that a financial advisor you already work with is a Bank On Yourself Authorized Advisor, e-mail info@bankon yourself.com and provide their full name and state.

*Make it a must that whenever you hear about something,
read or research something you think has value for your life,
don't let it become just knowledge.
Convert it into action,
for it is through our actions that our destiny is shaped.*
—TONY ROBBINS

*The best time to plant a tree is twenty years ago.
The second best time is today.*
—AFRICAN PROVERB

EPILOGUE

In chapter 1 of this book, I mentioned the firestorm of controversy surrounding Bank On Yourself by people who have heard that whole life insurance is a terrible place to put your money and are convinced that it must be a hoax—some new scheme for defrauding unwary people.

Much of this controversy is based on what financial advisors and insurance agents tell their clients about whole life being a terrible product, without any understanding of the little-known, special kind of policy we use for Bank On Yourself.

While working on this book, I began to wonder about the life insurance agents and financial advisors who have become Bank On Yourself Authorized Advisors. Before starting to work with B.O.Y., they had all heard the same kind of negative thinking—so what made them change their minds?

That change of attitude is even harder to make for two unexpected reasons: first, the many hours of additional training needed for a licensed insurance agent to master the concepts to become a B.O.Y. Authorized Advisor. And, even more important, he or she earns *much* smaller commissions from selling Bank On Yourself–type policies—primarily because, for the all-important paid-up additions rider component, the insurance companies pay the agent an almost negligible commission.

So why have these agents embraced Bank On Yourself? What convinced them it was a good thing, despite the prejudice they had acquired from all their earlier industry indoctrination against using whole life as a financial tool? And why would they embrace this approach when they make lower commissions? When I got a few of them together on a conference call and asked, some of the responses were surprising but revealing. (Out of fairness to the other two hundred–some B.O.Y. Advisors, I have not identified those whose comments are included here by their full names.)

Investigating Bank On Yourself

Russ: After working with whole life insurance in the beginning of my career, I got into the "buy term and invest the difference" idea. The belief was that whole life insurance was a lousy place to store money. We weren't thinking about financing, we were thinking about where you put money, and it wasn't going to be in a life insurance policy. People were saying, "Why would I want to do that?"

The conventional wisdom was if you need insurance coverage, let's buy the cheapest term insurance possible to serve the purpose and we'll invest the difference.

Before I even considered offering Bank On Yourself as a part of my practice, I spent about three months doing my own research. I went back and looked at everything that I could find to make sure that what I was being told was true. I had to get a comfort level for myself.

If it's so good, why haven't I heard about it before?
Jack: For me, when I ran across this, it slapped me in the face a little bit because I hadn't seen it. Nobody had taught me about this. How come this had never been presented to me? How come I didn't know anything about this?

I went on a mission to travel all across the country to find people that were doing this and tried to find holes in it. I wanted to find the holes. I wanted to see it as clearly as I could. I wanted criticism. I wanted critique. I wanted to find the problems, and I really couldn't find any.

The first thing I did, once I understood it, was implement my own policy in a pretty big way. I started a $60,000 annual premium policy for myself.

Russ: A lot of times when I'm interviewing with someone who has made an appointment to find out about Bank On Yourself, they bring up, "My biggest concern is that this is too good to be true. Why haven't I heard about it before?"

So what I relay to them is the three-month process that I went through myself, personally, as an experienced financial advisor and a licensed insurance broker/agent for many, many years and that I was stunned by the fact that this existed and actually was possible. I say, "If you think *you* are apprehensive, consider my situation where being in practice a very long time and then coming across this, I couldn't accept the fact that I didn't know about this sooner; so I had a high degree of skepticism."

What overcame his resistance?

Russ: One of the ways I finally came to grips with it is that I said, "Okay, let's break apart all the pieces of what I know about a cash value dividend-paying life insurance policy." I basically disassembled it and then reassembled it and verified each piece in my mind and said, okay, if I have a cash value policy, can I borrow the money out? The answer is yes.

So I went through that process with each individual component and verified each one. Once I did that, I was 100 percent convinced that everything I was being told about it was in fact true, because there was no way to refute it.

I couldn't believe that life insurance could be used in this fashion and that you could actually structure it in this way. The fact that you could use a life insurance policy as a personal source of financing—that was the thing that astonished me.

Why is it good business despite the reduced commissions?

Alan: There is a significant portion of the total premium that we get very little compensation on. With Bank On Yourself, on average we are taking a 50 percent pay cut versus traditional insurance. I talked to twenty-five advisors about joining my organization and about twenty-three of them right off the bat, the minute they heard that, said, "What do you mean, 'take a pay cut'? What's the matter with you?" Their minds clicked closed, and that was the end of it.

So why is this good business? For one thing, you create a client who is going to buy many more plans than somebody who bought traditional plans.

Clients quickly recognize the value of buying these policies. I have a client who bought twelve policies in two years. That would never happen with traditional life insurance.

The other factor is the referrals. Bank On Yourself Advisors get a lot more referrals without even asking for them, because people get so excited about this. Typically you almost never get a referral for life insurance.

How come I'm *not* nuts for doing this? The answer is all the referrals and because people buy more plans. The fact is that I do much greater volume of business.

Joe: I've heard the statistic that something like 95 percent of all the people that go into the life insurance business don't last much more than five years. It can be hard to keep clients. Just about everyone that got to be a client of mine over the years has previously had all kinds of disappointments with financial planning. So when people understand what Bank On Yourself can do for them, we know that there is not going to be a disappointment down the road. They are happier; they do more business with you. Just about everything else has more risk or is less worthwhile.

For me, it was that I didn't want to have to apologize to clients. That's the long story short.

David: When we were doing financial planning or investment planning during the bull market, we felt like king of the castle, right? Then when the markets tanked, who got blamed? *We* got blamed. Our clients love us when things are good. They blame us and they hate us when things are bad. With Bank On Yourself, the cash value doesn't go up one day and down the next.

When clients leave my office, people in the offices around me say that my clients are the happiest people they see. I've never really experienced that selling life insurance before. People are flocking to Bank On Yourself like there is no tomorrow.

ACKNOWLEDGMENTS

Writing a book you hope will be read by millions is a team project. I'd like to thank Dan Kennedy, from whom I have learned so much about business *and* life. Dan, it was you who taught me, "If you don't offend someone by noon each day, you're not doing much," words of wisdom that have given me the courage to forge ahead in my fight against ignorance and misinformation.

I am deeply grateful to Nelson Nash for his pioneering work over several decades with the Infinite Banking Concept. Nelson, you are a national treasure, and without you, this book would not exist. You have changed many lives, including my own, forever and for the better.

I owe enormous thanks to Lynn Kent for her untiring and invaluable assistance with the preparation of this book. And to Aurael Christall for her expert editorial support.

It was my husband, Larry Hayward, who first encouraged me to write this book and who has supported me lovingly and unselfishly in every way possible. I love and adore you, Larry, and appreciate your tolerance of the rather challenging aspects of my creative process and my admittedly quirky work habits.

Thanks also to Roger Bell and Gordon Golini, who have provided valuable technical support. If they ever got tired of my seemingly endless questions, they did not let it show.

I wish to thank the Bank On Yourself Authorized Advisors for their invaluable feedback and support in preparing this book. Their courage and dedication to pushing back the tide of ignorance surrounding B.O.Y. is inspiring. A very special thank-you goes to Scott Adamson, for his creativity, friendship, and unending support. Scott, thank you for being there for me! Without Tim Austin, the Bank On Yourself Authorized Advisor training program wouldn't exist. Thank you, Tim, for your integrity and expertise. You are truly one in a million!

I am profoundly grateful to my sister, Wendy Yellen, for her very valuable feedback on this book and for introducing me to Eidetics, a process that has helped me immensely in every way—physically, psychologically, emotionally, and spiritually. Thanks also to my Eidetic coaches, Leslie Dagnall and Dr. Akhter Ahsen.

This would be a very different book had it not been for the insightful contributions and talents of my collaborator, Bill Simon, who brought creativity and vitality to a subject that might otherwise have been a little dry. Bill, thanks for holding my feet to the fire, giving me brutally honest feedback, and helping turn this into a book that *far* exceeded my expectations.

A big thank-you goes to my brilliant book agent, Bill Gladstone, and his associate, Ming Russell, and to the team at Vanguard Publishing: Publisher Roger Cooper, for his vision in publishing a book that flies in the face of conventional wisdom; Associate Publisher Georgina Levitt; and the support of the Editorial and Marketing departments.

And last, but certainly not least, I wish to thank those who agreed to share the intimate details of their Bank On Yourself journeys in this book and the many folks who have implemented Bank On Yourself in their lives. Your willingness to keep an open mind and to look beyond the conventional thinking about money and finances is an inspiration to us all.

Free, No-Obligation Analysis Request Form

☐ Yes! I want to find out how to get back the money I pay for major purchases and grow wealth I can predict and count on. Please have a Bank On Yourself Authorized Advisor contact me so I can receive my free, no-obligation Bank On Yourself Analysis. I understand there will be *no* high pressure and I will *not* be asked to buy anything during this meeting. (Note: please *use black ink* for readability.)

Name: _____

Address: _____

City: _____ State: _____ Zip: _____

Day phone: _____ Eve. Phone: _____

Primary Email Address: _____

Best time to speak briefly during business hours: _____

NOTE: we *never* trade, rent, sell, or abuse your contact or other personal information. We ask for e-mail and phone to make it easy to put you in contact with the B.O.Y. Authorized Advisor we refer you to, who will prepare your analysis. By giving us this information, you authorize B.O.Y. and a B.O.Y. Advisor to contact you regarding your analysis.

Please tell us about you—this information will be held in *strict confidence*:

	You	*Spouse or Significant Other*
Age:	_____	_____
Occupation:	_____	_____
Annual Income:	_____	_____

Your biggest financial concern: _____

Do you own your home? _____ Approx. mortgage balance: _____

Approx. total credit card debt: _____ Interest rates: _____

Do you own a business? _____ If yes, what type: _____

If you were referred by a financial advisor, please list their name and state:

_____

To get maximum value from this meeting, we suggest you review the summary of B.O.Y. available free at www.BankOnYourselfFreeAnalysis.com.

How to arrange for your free B.O.Y. Analysis:
1. **Fax** this form to **(505) 466-2167** (no cover sheet necessary)
2. **Mail** to B.O.Y., 903 W. Alameda #526, Santa Fe, NM 87501
3. Or request it **online** at www.BankOnYourselfFreeAnalysis.com

FREE RESOURCES AND
RECOMMENDATIONS

Free Report and Newsletter!

To get a FREE report that summarizes how Bank On Yourself works, and a free subscription to the Bank On Yourself Success Tips e-zine (a $97 value), visit **www.BankOnYourself.com** and click on the "Free Special Report" button.

Additional Resources for Readers of this Book Are Available at www.BankOnYourself.com, including:

> ➤ Frequently asked questions
> ➤ Bank On Yourself success stories and testimonials
> ➤ Video presentations
> ➤ Blogs and podcasts
> ➤ Car buyers' resource packet
> ➤ Recommended reading and resources
> ➤ Calculators
> ➤ Articles and newsletter archive
> ➤ Upcoming workshops and public appearances

For Information On

Author Interviews and Public Appearances
To inquire about the availability of the author, Pamela Yellen, for interviews, teleconferences, speaking engagements, and other public appearances, please send details and your contact information to **media@bankonyourself.com**.

THE BANK ON YOURSELF AUTHORIZED
ADVISOR TRAINING PROGRAM

If, after reading this book, you think you might want to become a Bank On Yourself Authorized Advisor, here are a few things to consider:

Being a B.O.Y. Authorized Advisor is a challenging but very rewarding career. Challenging because, as you now know, Bank On Yourself goes against the grain of what Americans have been taught about money and finances, and because of the investment of time it takes to master the ins and outs of the concept, technical information, and plan design.

For those who stick with it, however, the rewards are many. Perhaps the greatest satisfaction comes from knowing you are changing your clients' lives by helping them achieve the financial peace of mind they seek and deserve.

Though there is a need for additional B.O.Y. Authorized Advisors throughout the United States and Canada, not everyone has what it takes to be successful with this, and not everyone is accepted into the training program.

If you have a life insurance license and at least one year of experience in financial services, you may qualify to be accepted into the Bank On Yourself Authorized Advisor training program. Please understand that it's not just past success that's considered. Attitude and a willingness to be mentored are key factors.

For details, and to be considered for the program, please go to **www.BankOnYourselfAdvisorInfo.com**.

Experience Pamela Yellen's *Other* "Secret Weapon"—FREE!

I'd like to ask you a personal question, if I may. . . .

How often do you experience joy . . . for no apparent reason at all?

I'm not just talking about contentment, or feeling okay about your life. I'm talking about pure, unadulterated feeling-like-you're-three-feet-off-the-ground *joy*! Perhaps you don't even believe it's possible . . . or that you deserve it.

If so, I can relate. Despite love and success, *parts* of my life still felt like a grind. I often procrastinated on critical things I needed to do for my business. I felt stressed much of the time. My perfectionism would make projects drag out much longer than I'd planned or expected. I wasn't fully *enjoying* all I had achieved.

All the strategies I used to try to break through these blocks worked—to a degree. But deep in my heart, I *knew* I could *be* more, *do* more, and *enjoy* my life more. I just couldn't seem to figure out how to get there. Maybe you can relate.

But friends were raving about the nearly instant breakthroughs they were having in their lives, using an extraordinary technology. And frankly, I was jealous! I was also skeptical but decided to give it a try. The shifts I experienced in so many different areas of my business and personal life were dramatic . . . and immediate.

Here are just a few: within *just one day*, some things that had seemed difficult and painful started feeling easy. Even effortless. Very quickly, situations that would normally stress me out suddenly simply stopped having that effect. Physical pain I'd had for more than a decade vanished. Perhaps the most unexpected benefit of all was the feeling of pure joy I began experiencing—even doing things I used to like least!

Are you—like myself—someone who wants to make and *even bigger* difference, a Ripple Maker™? If you are, I've arranged for you to get access to the internationally acclaimed expert in this technology (who also happens to be my sister, Wendy Yellen). Visit **www.Rediscover YourTruePower.com/boy** today and claim your Free Special Report and CD, "Pamela Yellen's Secret Weapon: The Breakthrough Technology to Rediscover Your True Personal Power."

GENERAL DISCLAIMER

All information in this book is provided "as is," with no guarantee of completeness, accuracy, or timeliness regarding the results obtained from the use of this information. And without warranty of any kind, express or implied, including, but not limited to warranties of performance, merchantability, and fitness for a particular purpose. Your use of this information is at your own risk. You assume full responsibility and risk of loss resulting from the use of this information. Pamela G. Yellen will not be liable for any direct, special, indirect, incidental, consequential, or punitive damages or any other damages whatsoever, whether in an action based upon a statute, contract, tort (including, but not limited to negligence), or otherwise, relating to the use of this information. In no event will Pamela G. Yellen, or Da Capo Press, or their related partnerships or corporations, or the partners, agents, or employees thereof be liable to you or anyone else for any decision made or action taken in reliance on the information in this book or for any consequential, special, or similar damages, even if advised of the possibility of such damages.

Neither Pamela G. Yellen nor Da Capo Press is engaged in rendering legal, accounting, or other professional services. If accounting, financial, legal, or tax advice is required, the services of a competent professional should be sought.

Information that was accurate as of the time of publication may become outdated by marketplace changes or conditions, new or revised laws, or other circumstances. Any slights against individuals, companies, or organizations are unintentional. All figures and examples in the book are based on rates and assumptions no later in time than July 2008, thus, these rates and assumptions are not guaranteed and may be subject to change. As in all assumptions and examples, individual results may vary based on a wide range of factors unique to each person's situation.